LIGUORI CATHOLIC

The Gospel *of* Mark

REVEALING THE MYSTERY OF JESUS

WILLIAM A. ANDERSON, DMIN, PHD

Liguori
LIGUORI, MISSOURI

Imprimi Potest: Harry Grile, CSsR, Provincial
Denver Province, The Redemptorists

Printed with Ecclesiastical Permission and Approved for Private or Instructional Use

Nihil Obstat: Rev. Msgr. Kevin Michael Quirk, JCD, JV
                Censor Librorum

Imprimatur: + Michael J. Bransfield
              Bishop of Wheeling-Charleston
January 6, 2012

Published by Liguori Publications
Liguori, Missouri 63057

To order, call 800-325-9521
www.liguori.org

Library of Congress Cataloging-in-Publication Data
Anderson, William Angor, 1937-
    The gospel of Mark : revealing the mystery of Jesus / William A. Anderson. — 1st ed.
      p. cm.
    ISBN 978-0-7648-2121-9
    1. Bible. N.T. Mark—Textbooks. 2. Bible. N.T. Mark—Commentaries. I. Title.
    BS2586.A53 2012
    226.30071--dc23

                                                      2012004449

Liguori Publications, a nonprofit corporation, is an apostolate of the Redemptorists. To learn more about the Redemptorists, visit Redemptorists.com.

Printed in the United States of America
16 15 14 13 12 / 5 4 3 2 1
First Edition

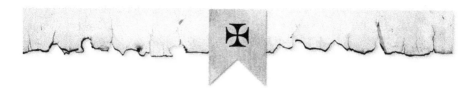

Contents

Acknowledgments 7

Introduction to *Liguori Catholic Bible Study* 9
Group and Individual Study 10

***Lectio Divina* (Sacred Reading) 11**

How to Use This Bible-Study Companion 14
A Process for Sacred Reading 15
Group-Study Formats 16

Introduction: The Gospel of Mark 19

Lesson 1   Preparation for Jesus' Public Ministry 25
Group Study (Mark 1:1–13) 26

Lesson 2   The Mystery of Jesus 33
Part 1: Group Study (Mark 1:14–45) 34
Part 2: Individual Study (Mark 2—3:6) 41

Lesson 3   The Mystery of the Reign of God 49
Part 1: Group Study (Mark 4:35—5) 50
Part 2: Individual Study (Mark 3:7—4:34) 55

Lesson 4   The Power of Faith 66
Part 1: Group Study (Mark 6) 67
Part 2: Individual Study (Mark 7—8:26) 74

Lesson 5   Revealing the Mystery 82
Part 1: Group Study (Mark 8:27—9:8) 83
Part 2: Individual Study (Mark 9:9–32) 88

Lesson 6   The Mystery Fully Revealed   92

      Part 1: Group Study (Mark 9:33—10:12)   93

      Part 2: Individual Study (Mark 10:13–52)   99

Lesson 7   Jesus in Jerusalem   106

      Part 1: Group Study (Mark 11—12:12)   108

      Part 2: Individual Study (Mark 12:13—13)   115

Lesson 8   Jesus' Passion and Resurrection   122

      Part 1: Group Study (Mark 15:21—16)   124

      Part 2: Individual Study (Mark 14—15:20)   132

> NOTE: The length of each Bible section varies. Group leaders should combine sections as needed to fit the number of sessions in their program.

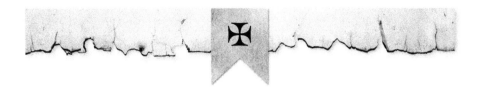

Dedication

This series is lovingly dedicated to the memory of my parents, Kathleen and Angor Anderson, in gratitude for all they shared with all who knew them, especially my siblings and me.

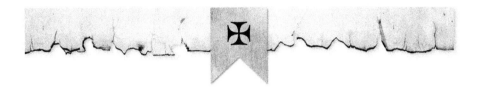

Acknowledgments

Bible studies and reflections depend on the help of others who read the manuscript and make suggestions. I am especially indebted to Sister Anne Francis Bartus, CSJ, DMin, whose vast experience and knowledge were very helpful in bringing this series to its final form.

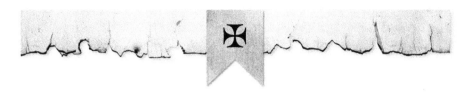

Introduction to
Liguori Catholic Bible Study

READING THE BIBLE can be daunting. It's a complex book, and many a person of goodwill has tried to read the Bible and ended up putting it down in utter confusion. It helps to have a companion, and _Liguori Catholic Bible Study_ is a solid one. Over the course of this series, you'll learn about biblical messages, themes, personalities, and events and understand how the books of the Bible rose out of the need to address new situations.

Across the centuries, people of faith have asked, "Where is God in this moment?" Millions of Catholics look to the Bible for encouragement in their journey of faith. Wisdom teaches us not to undertake Bible study alone, disconnected from the Church that was given Scripture to share and treasure. When used as a source of prayer and thoughtful reflection, the Bible comes alive.

Your choice of a Bible-study program should be dictated by what you want to get out of it. One goal of _Liguori Catholic Bible Study_ is to give readers greater familiarity with the Bible's structure, themes, personalities, and message. But that's not enough. This program will also teach you to use Scripture in your prayer. God's message is as compelling and urgent today as ever, but we get only part of the message when it's memorized and stuck in our heads. It's meant for the entire person—physical, emotional, and spiritual.

We're baptized into life with Christ, and we're called to live more fully with Christ today as we practice the values of justice, peace, forgiveness, and community. God's new covenant was written on the hearts of the people of Israel; we, their spiritual descendants, are loved that intimately by God today. _Liguori Catholic Bible Study_ will draw you closer to God, in whose image and likeness we are fashioned.

Group and Individual Study

The *Liguori Catholic Bible Study* series is intended for group and individual study and prayer. This series gives you the tools to start a study group. Gathering two or three people in a home or announcing the meeting of a Bible-study group in a parish or community can bring surprising results. Each lesson in this series contains a section to help groups study, reflect, pray, and share biblical reflections. Each lesson also has a second section for individual study.

Many people who want to learn more about the Bible don't know where to begin. This series gives them a place to start and helps them continue until they're familiar with all the books of the Bible.

Bible study can be a lifelong project, always enriching those who wish to be faithful to God's Word. When people complete a study of the whole Bible, they can begin again, making new discoveries with each new adventure into the Word of God.

Lectio Divina
(Sacred Reading)

BIBLE STUDY isn't just a matter of gaining intellectual knowledge of the Bible; it's also about gaining a greater understanding of God's love and concern for creation. The purpose of reading and knowing the Bible is to enrich our relationship with God. God loves us and gave us the Bible to illustrate that love. As Pope Benedict XVI reminds us, a study of the Bible is not only an intellectual pursuit but also a spiritual adventure that should influence our dealings with God and neighbor.

The Meaning of *Lectio Divina*

Lectio divina is a Latin expression that means "divine or sacred reading." The process for *lectio divina* consists of Scripture readings, reflection, and prayer. Many clergy, religious, and laity use *lectio divina* in their daily spiritual reading to develop a closer and more loving relationship with God. Learning about Scripture has as its purpose the living of its message, which demands a period of reflection on the Scripture passages.

Prayer and *Lectio Divina*

Prayer is a necessary element for the practice of *lectio divina*. The entire process of reading and reflecting is a prayer. It's not merely an intellectual pursuit; it's also a spiritual one. Page 18 includes an Opening Prayer for gathering one's thoughts before moving on to the passages in each section. This prayer may be used privately or in a group. For those who use the book for daily spiritual reading, the prayer for each section may be repeated each day. Some may wish to keep a journal of each day's meditation.

Pondering the Word of God

Lectio divina is the ancient Christian spiritual practice of reading the holy Scriptures with intentionality and devotion. This practice helps Christians center themselves and descend to the level of the heart to enter an inner quiet space, finding God.

This sacred reading is distinct from reading for knowledge or information, and it's more than the pious practice of spiritual reading. It is the practice of opening ourselves to the action and inspiration of the Holy Spirit. As we intentionally focus on and become present to the inner meaning of the Scripture passage, the Holy Spirit enlightens our minds and hearts. We come to the text willing to be influenced by a deeper meaning that lies within the words and thoughts we ponder.

In this space, we open ourselves to be challenged and changed by the inner meaning we experience. We approach the text in a spirit of faith and obedience as a disciple ready to be taught by the Holy Spirit. As we savor the sacred text, we let go of our usual control of how we expect God to act in our lives and surrender our hearts and consciences to the flow of the divine (*divina*) through the reading (*lectio*).

The fundamental principle of *lectio divina* leads us to understand the profound mystery of the Incarnation, "The Word became flesh," not only in history but also within us.

Praying *Lectio* Today

Before you begin, relax your body and maintain a posture of prayer (back straight, eyes shut, feet flat on the floor). Then practice these four simple actions:

1. Read a passage from Scripture or the daily Mass readings. This is known as *lectio*. (If the Word of God is read aloud, the hearers listen attentively.)

2. Pray the selected passage with attention as you listen for a specific meaning that comes to mind. Once again, the reading is listened to or silently read and reflected or meditated on. This is known as *meditatio*.

3. The exercise becomes active. Pick a word, sentence, or idea that surfaces from your consideration of the chosen text. Does the reading remind you of a person, place, or experience? If so, pray about it. Compose your thoughts and reflection into a simple word or phrase. This prayer-thought will help you remove distractions during the *lectio*. This exercise is called *oratio*.

4. In silence, with your eyes closed, quiet yourself and become conscious of your breathing. Let your thoughts, feelings, and concerns fade as you consider the selected passage in the previous step (*oratio*). If you're distracted, use your prayer word to help you return to silence. This is *contemplatio*.

This exercise can take as long as you want, but in the context of this Bible study, 10 to 20 minutes should be sufficient.

Many teachers of prayer call contemplation the prayer of resting in God, a prelude to losing oneself in the presence of God. Scripture is transformed in our hearing as we pray and allow our hearts to unite intimately with the Lord. The Word truly takes on flesh, and this time it is manifested in our flesh.

How to Use This
Bible-Study Companion

THE BIBLE, along with the commentaries and reflections found in this study, will help participants become familiar with the Scripture texts and lead them to reflect more deeply on the texts' message. At the end of this study, participants will have a firm grasp of the Gospel of Mark and realize how that gospel offers spiritual nourishment. This study is not only an intellectual adventure, it's also a spiritual one. The reflections lead participants into their own journey with the Scripture readings.

Context

When each author wrote his gospel, he didn't simply link random stories about Jesus—he placed them in a context that often stressed a message. To help readers learn about each passage in relation to those around it, each lesson begins with an overview that puts the Scripture passages into context.

Part 1—Group Study

To give participants a comprehensive study of the Gospel of Mark, the book is divided into 8 lessons. Lesson 1 is group study only; Lessons 2 through 8 are divided into Part 1, group study; and Part 2, individual study. For example, Lesson 2 covers passages from Mark 1:14–3:6. The study group reads and discusses only Mark 1:14–45 (Part 1). Participants privately read and reflect on Mark 2–3:6 (Part 2).

Group study may or may not include *lectio divina*. With *lectio divina*, the group meets for ninety minutes using the first format on page 16. Otherwise the group meets for one hour using the second format on page 16, and participants are urged to privately read the *lectio divina* section at the end of Part 1. It contains additional reflections on the Scripture passages studied during the group session that will take participants even further into the passages.

Part 2—Individual Study

The gospel passages not covered in Part 1 are divided into three to six shorter components, one to be studied each day. Participants who don't belong to a study group can use the lessons for private sacred reading. They may choose to reflect on one Scripture passage per day, making it possible for a clearer understanding of the Scripture passages used in their *lectio divina* (sacred reading).

A PROCESS FOR SACRED READING

Liguori Publications has designed this study to be user friendly and manageable. However, group dynamics and leaders vary. We're not trying to keep the Holy Spirit from working in your midst, thus we suggest you decide beforehand which format works best for your group. If you have limited time, you could study the Bible as a group and save prayer and reflection for personal time.

However, if your group wishes to digest and feast on sacred Scripture through both prayer and study, we recommend you spend closer to ninety minutes each week by gathering to study and pray with Scripture. *Lectio divina* (see page 11) is an ancient contemplative prayer form that moves readers from the head to the heart in meeting the Lord. We strongly suggest using this prayer form whether in individual or group study.

GROUP-STUDY FORMATS

1. Bible Study With *Lectio Divina*

About ninety minutes of group study

- ✠ Gathering and opening prayer (3–5 minutes)
- ✠ Scripture passage read aloud (5 minutes)
- ✠ Silently review the commentary and prepare to discuss it with the group (3-5 minutes)
- ✠ Discuss the Scripture passage along with the commentary and reflection (30 minutes)
- ✠ Scripture passage read aloud a second time, followed by quiet time for meditation and contemplation (5 minutes)
- ✠ Spend some time in prayer with the selected passage. Group participants will slowly read the Scripture passage a third time in silence, listening for the voice of God as they read (10–20 minutes)
- ✠ Shared reflection (10–15 minutes)
- ✠ Closing prayer (3–5 minutes)

To become acquainted with lectio divina, *see page 11.*

2. Bible Study

About one hour of group study

- ✠ Gathering and opening prayer (3–5 minutes)
- ✠ Scripture passage read aloud (5 minutes)
- ✠ Silently review the commentary and prepare to discuss it with the group (3–5 minutes)
- ✠ Discuss the Scripture passage along with the commentary and reflection (40 minutes)
- ✠ Closing prayer (3–5 minutes)

Notes to the Leader

✠ Bring a copy of the *New American Bible,* revised edition.

✠ Plan which sections will be covered each week.

✠ Read the material in advance of each session.

✠ Establish written ground rules. (Example: We won't keep you longer than ninety minutes; don't dominate the sharing by arguing or debating.)

✠ Meet in an appropriate and welcoming gathering space (church building, meeting room, house).

✠ Provide name tags and perhaps use a brief icebreaker for the first meeting; ask participants to introduce themselves.

✠ Mark the Scripture passage(s) that will be read during the session.

✠ Decide how you would like the Scripture to be read aloud (whether by one or multiple readers).

✠ Use a clock or watch.

✠ Provide extra Bibles (or copies of the Scripture passages) for participants who don't bring their Bible.

✠ Ask participants to read "Introduction: The Gospel of Mark" (page 19) before the first session.

✠ Tell participants which passages to study and urge them to read the passages and commentaries before the meeting.

✠ If you opt to use the *lectio divina* format, familiarize yourself with this prayer form ahead of time.

Notes to Participants

✠ Bring a copy of the *New American Bible,* revised edition.

✠ Read "Introduction: The Gospel of Mark" (page 19) before the first class.

✠ Read the Scripture passages and commentary before each session.

✠ Be prepared to share and listen respectfully. (This is not a time to debate beliefs or argue.)

Opening Prayer

Leader: O God, come to my assistance,

Response: O Lord, make haste to help me.

Leader: Glory be to the Father, and to the Son, and to the Holy Spirit...

Response: ...as it was in the beginning, is now, and ever shall be, world without end. Amen.

Leader: Christ is the vine, and we are the branches. As branches linked to Jesus, the vine, we are called to recognize that the Scriptures are always being fulfilled in our lives. It is the living Word of God living on in us. Come Holy Spirit, fill the hearts of your faithful, and kindle in us the fire of your divine wisdom, knowledge, and love.

Response: Open our minds and hearts as we study your great love for us as shown in the Bible.

Reader: (Open your Bible to the assigned Scripture(s) and read in a paced, deliberate manner. Pause for one minute, listening for that word, phrase, or image that you may use in your *lectio divina* practice.)

Closing Prayer

Leader: Let us pray as Jesus taught us.

Response: Our Father...

Leader: Lord, inspire us with your Spirit as we study your Word in the Bible. Be with us this day and every day as we strive to know you and serve you and to love as you love. We believe that through your goodness and love, the Spirit of the Lord is truly upon us. Allow the words of the Bible, your Word, to capture us and inspire us to live as you live and to love as you love.

Response: Amen.

Leader: May the divine assistance remain always with us.

Response: In the name of the Father, and of the Son, and of the Holy Spirit. Amen.

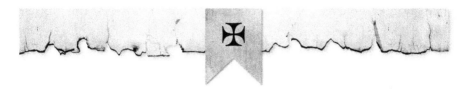

INTRODUCTION

The Gospel of Mark

Read this overview before the first class.

A disciple of a renowned and holy abbot borrowed a copy of an abbot's personal journal, read it, and returned it to the abbot, expressing his admiration for the abbot and boasting that he had memorized all the pages of the journal so he could repeat them to the other disciples. He believed the other disciples would certainly admire him for his ability to memorize the journal and admire the abbot for his deeply spiritual reflections. The abbot looked sadly on his disciple and said, "The journal was not meant to be about me, but about you. You missed the whole purpose of my sharing the journal with you."

Although the Bible is the Word of God, it's not only about God and God's dealings with the people of the past—it's about us. As we understand the Bible more fully, we understand its application to our lives more deeply. In this text, the commentary and reflection should be seen not only as a message about Jesus, but also as a message about our life in our relationship with God.

Who Was Mark?

"Mark my words" is an old expression. In a sense, it's easier to mark Mark's words than it is to mark Mark. The problem of knowing who Mark is comes from an acceptable custom in the early Church period of using the name of a famous disciple of Jesus to give more authority and credibility to a manuscript. The problem with naming the author of the Gospel of Mark is that he did not seem to have the authority of the other disciples mentioned as companions of Jesus. If an author other than

Mark wrote the gospel, he certainly wouldn't have chosen to call himself Mark, because that name would have carried little authority outside the circle of those immediately associated with him. So, surprising as it may sound, most commentators feel that Mark is the true name of the author of this gospel, simply because a writer with a different name would not have chosen Mark.

A second-century document written by a bishop named Papias quotes an earlier document written by a man named John the Presbyter, who identifies Mark as the author of this gospel. According to John the Presbyter, Mark was a companion and interpreter for Peter, who writes, "The chosen one at Babylon sends you greeting, as does Mark, my son" (1 Peter 5:13). Some believe Mark received his knowledge about Jesus from Peter. Mark's name, however, surfaces in other areas of the Scriptures. The Acts of the Apostles reports that Peter sought out the house of Mark's mother after being freed from prison by an angel (12:1–12). The house seemed to have been a gathering place for some members of the early Church community. From this passage of Acts, we know again that Peter had some contact with a man named John Mark.

Later in Acts, we read of young man named John Mark who accompanied Paul and Barnabas on their first missionary journey, but Mark left them for some unexplained reason (13:13). When Mark sought to join them at a later date, Paul refused to accept him as a companion because of Mark's sudden departure during their first missionary journey. Barnabas and Paul had a heated argument over this and separated, leaving Mark as a companion of Barnabas (15:36–40). Later, in a letter to the Colossians, Paul named Mark as a companion and a cousin of Barnabas (4:10). In all these references to Mark, two questions arise. First, were these references to Mark all to the same person, and second, is he the one who wrote the gospel?

We can say that the name of the author may really have been Mark, but we still have the question "Who is Mark?" In the final analysis, all we can say is that evidence leans in the direction that someone named Mark is the author of this gospel.

When Was the Gospel of Mark Written?

Because we don't have a recorded date for this gospel, we must look at the gospel itself and try to discover references that might point out the date of its composition. Within the gospel, we find a reference to the desecration of the Temple, which took place during the Romans' destruction of Jerusalem (13:14). Mark seems to know something about the siege of Jerusalem, which lasted from 66 to 70, but he doesn't demonstrate as much knowledge of the destruction of Jerusalem as do the authors of Matthew or Luke. For this reason, commentators place the writing of the Gospel of Mark somewhere between the years 66 to 70, which makes it the earliest gospel written. The authors of Matthew and Luke, who wrote in about 85, were able to use Mark's Gospel as a resource for their own gospels.

Mark's Genius

For many years after Jesus' resurrection, the disciples traveled through villages and towns preaching about Jesus' life and message. Some told stories based on Jesus' actions during his life, and others shared Jesus' sayings. Mark listened to these messages and memorized many of them. If he was a companion of Peter's, he would have learned a great deal from Peter. If he was the Mark identified as the son of the woman named Mary who received Peter into her house after he escaped from prison, he would have learned from Peter and the others who had gathered to pray at Mary's home. If he was John Mark, the companion of Paul and Barnabas, he would have heard many accounts of Jesus' life and message and most likely would himself have preached about Jesus.

Before Mark wrote about the preaching of the early Church in an orderly presentation, the gospel consisted almost entirely of the spoken message about Jesus the Christ and his teachings. Mark did not and could not write a biography of Jesus because, like all gospel writers, he's proclaiming a message he received from other disciples who reflected as a community on Jesus' life and message after his resurrection. The genius of Mark is that he received a theological message about Jesus and placed Jesus' sayings and the events of his life in historical sequence. Therefore, Mark wrote the first gospel.

Why Did Mark Write His Gospel?

Shortly after early Church members began spreading Jesus' message, they encountered hostility and persecution, especially at home in Jerusalem and later in Rome. After Jesus' resurrection, the disciples—once a frightened group of Jesus' followers—suddenly became so enthused by Jesus' life, message, and resurrection that they were willing to travel far to spread his message.

They weren't always welcomed in many of the places they preached, and eventually they were persecuted and killed for preaching about Christ and rejecting the gods of the nations they visited. The Romans mistrusted these followers of Christ who refused to join the army, attend the killing games taking place in the Coliseum, or worship the gods of Rome, especially the emperor. The two outstanding leaders among the disciples, Peter and Paul, were killed in Rome around 64, shortly before Mark wrote his gospel. Many other martyrs joined Peter and Paul, accepting death rather than denying Christ. Unfortunately, as happens during periods of persecution, many people became *apostates*, preserving their lives by denying Christ. Mark wrote his gospel in the midst of this turmoil to encourage and instruct Christ's suffering and dying followers.

This persecution caused some members of the early Church to question the reason for this suffering. Mark, through his gospel, said their suffering was the path of discipleship. If Jesus suffered for the sake of the kingdom, his followers must do the same. The call to discipleship is a call to imitate Jesus even in his suffering and death. Mark has Jesus himself tell these disciples the full meaning of discipleship: "Whoever wishes to come after me must deny himself, take up his cross, and follow me" (8:34). The example and words of Jesus are not for his generation alone. Mark recognizes that they are meant for all generations. He encourages the people to make sense of their suffering and death by keeping their eyes on Christ, the perfect person who suffered and died for them. Mark understood the urgency of sharing this message with Jesus' followers, who were suffering in Rome and elsewhere.

Another reason for Mark to write a gospel was the aging of Jesus' original followers. At some point, the message had to be written before all Jesus' followers died. The message of Jesus' life and teachings would be preserved more faithfully if someone recorded it. To help followers remain faithful to the original teachings and events of Jesus' life, Mark wrote his gospel. Because Mark was closer in time to the events of Jesus' life, he presents a more human—and even weaker—image of Jesus and his disciples than the other three gospel writers did.

What Are Some Characteristics of Mark's Gospel?

Because the Gospel of Mark was a source for the Gospels of Matthew and Luke (see "The Synoptic Gospels" in the introductory book of this series, *Introduction to the Bible*), many characteristics of Mark's Gospel appear in the Gospels of Matthew and Luke, but they sometimes emphasize a different message. In investigating how Matthew and Luke apply the Gospel of Mark to their gospels, readers can better understand the authors' purpose in writing their gospels (see "Redaction Criticism" in *Introduction to the Bible*).

The Messianic Secret

When Mark identifies Jesus as the Christ in the first sentence of his gospel, he reveals he's writing about Jesus as the early Church understood him after his resurrection. In other words, he is writing as a follower of Christ who already knows the end of the story. Because he is writing for a Greek audience, Mark chooses the Greek title for Messiah at the outset of his gospel, the title *Christ*. Mark is writing about Jesus *the Christ*, who suffered, died, and was raised.

Although Jesus was indeed the Christ, Mark notes Jesus' reaction to the demons who try to identify him. When Jesus casts out demons, the demons identify him as the Messiah, and Jesus immediately commands them to be silent. Mark writes, "He cured many who were sick with various diseases, and he drove out many demons, not permitting them to speak because they knew him" (1:34). When Jesus heals someone, Jesus tells the person not to spread the news about the miracle, but unlike the demons who must obey Jesus, human beings have free will and spread the news of Jesus' miracles anyway.

Jesus' effort to keep his miracles and power over demons a secret is known to commentators as the "messianic secret," which is found predominately in the Gospel of Mark. Why Jesus wishes to keep his identity hidden is a question many commentators have tried to answer. Many people expected a warrior-type Messiah, which Jesus was not. In Jesus' day, Roman authorities didn't look kindly on those who claimed to be the Messiah, because some of the people were awaiting a Messiah who would lead them in a battle against their enemies. Jesus would have wanted to freely preach his message without being a threat to religious leaders and Roman rulers. Mark recognized that Jesus became the Christ through his resurrection when he overcame death and brought spiritual salvation to all people.

Jesus, the Son of God

In the first line of his gospel, Mark identifies Jesus as the Son of God. Throughout the gospel, Jesus performs miracles that clearly belong to God alone—walking on water, calming storms, and forgiving sins. The great power over demons strongly underlines Jesus' divine power. Mark explicitly refers to Jesus as the Son of God in only a few sections (1:1, 9:7, 15:39), choosing instead to show Jesus in this light through his miracles and through the disciples' struggle to understand Jesus and his message.

The Meaning of Discipleship

Mark, who is writing closest in time to the lives of Jesus and his disciples, has no difficulty presenting Jesus' disciples as typical and weak human beings. They misunderstand Jesus, frustrate him, miss some of the obvious points of his message, and abandon him during his passion. In the later gospels, the disciples—although still identified as struggling human beings—receive a little more respect.

The true disciple is one who follows Jesus' example and who suffers and willingly accepts death for the sake of the kingdom. The disciples should not look for glory, but for a cross in this life. They should pick up their own crosses and follow Jesus. For those who remain faithful, an eternal reward awaits. The Gospel of Mark stresses the true notion of discipleship, a central theme of this gospel written for Christians suffering persecution in Rome.

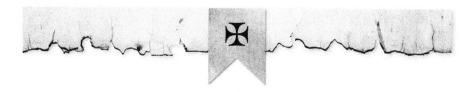

Preparation for Jesus' Public Ministry

MARK 1:1–13

On coming up out of the water he saw the heavens being torn open and the Spirit, like a dove, descending upon him. And a voice came from the heavens, "You are my beloved Son; with you I am well pleased." (1:10–11)

Opening Prayer (SEE PAGE 18)

Context

Mark's Gospel begins by stating that Jesus is the Christ, the Son of God. John the Baptist comes to prepare the way of the Lord as foretold by the prophets. John declares that Jesus is greater than he: John baptizes with water, but Jesus baptizes with water *and* the Spirit. When Jesus comes out of the water, the Spirit comes upon Jesus like a dove, and a voice from heaven declares that Jesus is God's beloved Son. The Spirit drives Jesus into the desert, where he remains for forty days and is tempted by Satan.

GROUP STUDY (MARK 1:1–13)

Read Mark 1:1–13 aloud.

1:1 *Jesus Christ, the Son of God*

Mark introduces his gospel by proclaiming abruptly that this is "The beginning of the gospel of Jesus Christ [the Son of God]." Many commentators believe the first line of the Gospel of Mark is actually the title of the gospel. More recent translations place "the Son of God" in brackets to note that the phrase is missing from certain important manuscripts.

Mark, like the other gospel writers, knows the end of the story: Jesus died and was raised, he is the Christ, and he is the Son of God. Mark recognizes God's expansive love revealed through the events of Jesus' life, death, and resurrection. The call to discipleship, which lies at the center of his gospel, presents Jesus Christ as the prime example of discipleship. Later, Mark quotes Jesus as saying that the true disciple must deny oneself, take up one's cross, and "follow me" (8:34).

Mark refers to his writing as a *Gospel*, the Good News of Jesus Christ the Son of God. When we look at all Jesus suffered in spreading his message, we wonder how Mark can call this Good News. The Good News, however, isn't the life and message alone, but also the outcome—the resurrection, which brings us salvation. Those persecuted for the sake of Christ can also view *their* suffering as good news: Like Christ, they bring blessings on themselves and God's creation, and they will also be raised in glory.

Saint Paul the apostle's letters speak of remaining faithful to the gospel, but he spoke his message before Mark wrote the first gospel. When Paul spoke of the Good News of Jesus Christ, he wasn't referring to a book, but to the preached message. Just as the early disciples had the Good News to preach, Mark preaches the Good News of Jesus Christ, the Son of God, to encourage the suffering Christians to remain faithful and trusting.

Toward the end of Mark's Gospel, when Jesus dies on the cross, Mark tells us that a centurion declares, "Truly this man was the Son of God!" (15:39). This is the theme of Mark's Gospel: Jesus is indeed the Christ, but we shouldn't overlook the truth that he is also the Son of God.

The story of the Gospel is a story of God's love for all people. Christians today can proclaim they believe Jesus is the Christ, the Son of God. In reality, however, we may be no different than the disciples of Jesus' day. Throughout Mark's narrative, Jesus' disciples struggle to understand Jesus and his message and its application to their lives. Although we today can agree that Jesus is the Christ, the Son of God, we can also experience a struggle similar to that of Jesus' immediate disciples. We know it, we believe it, yet we still ponder this astounding truth.

1:2–8 The Preaching of John the Baptist

John the Baptist appears in the desert, preaching a baptism of repentance that leads to the forgiveness of sins. Mark uses a quotation he identifies as coming from Isaiah the prophet but which is actually a collection of three Old Testament quotations from Malachi, Isaiah, and Exodus. Malachi writes, "Now I am sending my messenger—he will prepare the way before me" (3:1). In Isaiah we read, "A voice proclaims: In the wilderness prepare the way of the LORD! Make straight in the wasteland a highway for our God!" (40:3). In Exodus we read, "See, I am sending an angel before you, to guard you on the way and bring you to the place I have prepared. Be attentive to him and obey him" (23:20–21). Joined as one in Mark's Gospel, the quotations proclaim that before the Messiah (*Christ* in Greek) comes, God is sending a messenger to prepare the way of the Lord.

Just as God sends John the Baptist to prepare the way of the Lord, the prophets of the Old Testament prepare the way for John by announcing that a messenger, a voice in the wasteland, will prepare the way of the Lord. John preaches in the desert, a place that held many symbols for the people of Jesus' day. The Judeans recalled that the desert is where the Israelites spent forty years on their journey with Moses toward the Promised Land. In the desert, God visited the "chosen people" and spoke to the prophets. The desert was also aligned with evil, known as the place demons dwelt, which would explain why Jesus had to face his temptations in the desert. The saints often spoke of losing an experience of God as a desert experience, a dark night of the soul. It was often a time filled with dryness and overwhelming temptation. They were facing their demons, but with the help of God they, like Jesus, remained faithful.

John preaches a baptism of repentance, namely a call to change one's life, which leads to the forgiveness of sin. Although John preaches in the desert, he baptizes in the Jordan. Mark isn't as familiar with the geography of Palestine as Matthew was, and he mistakenly places the desert and the Jordan together.

When the people listen to John, they resolve to avoid sinfulness, and they accept baptism as a sign of their commitment to a new life. Mark exaggerates when he states that all the people of the countryside and Jerusalem come out to be baptized by John. Mark's message is that a large number of people will come to Jesus through the preaching of the Baptist.

John the Baptist lived a life of austerity in the desert, possibly as a member of a group known as the Essenes. A branch of the Essenes withdrew into the desert near the Dead Sea, south of Palestine, to live in prayer and sacrifice as they awaited the imminent coming of the Christ. They believed the Messiah would need disciples who remained faithful and dedicated to Jewish laws and customs. Being in the desert, they had to eat what they could find. John survived on grasshoppers and wild honey. Many practiced celibacy and, like John, wore rough and uncomfortable clothing resembling that of Elijah the prophet, who is described as wearing "a hairy garment with a leather belt around his waist" (2 Kings 1:8). Later in the Gospel of Mark, Jesus refers to John the Baptist when he announces that Elijah has come.

After Jesus' resurrection, some of John the Baptist's followers believed that John, not Jesus, was the Christ. John baptized Jesus; therefore, he must be greater than Jesus. Mark subtly refutes this argument by having John himself proclaim that the one who is to come after him—Jesus—is more powerful than John, so powerful and worthy of respect that the Baptist isn't even worthy to untie Jesus' sandals. In Jewish households, slaves untied guests' sandals. John's baptism calls those receiving it to repentance, whereas Jesus' baptism is far greater: Jesus will baptize in the Holy Spirit.

The baptism John performed was not a sacramental baptism, but a baptism of commitment. Those who accepted the Baptist's call to repentance publicly affirmed this call by allowing John to baptize them. It was a visible sign of an interior change of life. John points beyond repentance and forgiveness to the one mightier than he.

1:9–11 The Baptism of Jesus

Jesus stands in the crowd awaiting his turn to be baptized by John. Until now, Mark has named only the people of Judea and Jerusalem as coming for John's baptism, but now Jesus arrives from his hometown of Nazareth in Galilee, an area north of Judea and Jerusalem. Mark states simply that Jesus was baptized by John. Many commentators note that the sinless Jesus, in accepting a baptism of repentance for the forgiveness of sin, takes upon himself the sins of all people. He comes, not in his own name, but as the Savior of all. Jesus expresses God's great love for all people as he now begins his public ministry, which will eventually lead to his death and resurrection. Taking upon himself the sins of all doesn't end with Jesus' baptism and is a sign of future events suffered on behalf of all people.

When Jesus comes out of the water after John baptizes him, the heavens are torn asunder and a dove settles on Jesus, symbolizing the power of the Spirit coming upon him. The tearing open of the heavens is a reference from Isaiah, a call for God's favor on a people who return from the Babylonian exile. Isaiah writes, "Oh, that you would rend the heavens and come down, with the mountains quaking before you" (63:19). A voice addresses Jesus from the heavens, proclaiming that Jesus is God's "beloved Son" (1:11), which is another way of saying God's only Son. The voice is apparently heard only by Jesus and passed on to the reader by Mark.

The Holy Spirit's descent on Jesus designates Jesus' anointing for his mission as found in Isaiah the prophet, who proclaims in God's name: "Here is my servant whom I uphold, my chosen one with whom I am pleased. Upon him I have put my spirit" (42:1). In aligning the event with Isaiah's words, Mark portrays Jesus as the servant Messiah. In Acts of the Apostles, when Peter is preaching at the house of Cornelius, he speaks about "how God anointed Jesus of Nazareth with the holy Spirit and power" (10:38), an allusion to Jesus' baptism at the Jordan.

Mark presents an image of the Trinity in this passage. The voice from heaven is that of God the Father, the beloved Son is God the Son, and the Holy Spirit is God the Holy Spirit. All three appear in this passage. The notion of the Trinity took as many centuries to understand in the early

Church as the understanding of the unity of the humanity and divinity of Jesus did. When Mark wrote his gospel, the word *Trinity* in reference to God the Father, God the Son, and God the Holy Spirit wasn't yet used.

1:12–13 The Temptation of Jesus

Mark shows the influence of the Holy Spirit in Jesus' life as the Spirit "drove him out into the desert." The Spirit's power in Jesus' life shows how the Spirit works in ours. Jesus spends forty days in the desert, where he is tempted by Satan. The forty days are reminiscent of the forty years the Israelites spent in the desert during the Exodus and of Elijah's journey of forty days and nights to Mount Horeb (1 Kings 19:8). Mark says no more about the temptations—he simply says Jesus was tempted. Jesus spent the period in the desert facing roaming wild beasts and temptation by Satan. Mark tells us that angels ministered to Jesus, a message that is also reminiscent of angels' ministering to Elijah in the desert (1 Kings 19:5). Although Mark doesn't tell of the individual temptations and the final outcome, the angels' ministry implies that Jesus successfully overcame Satan's temptations.

Review Questions

1. What title does Mark give his gospel, and what is significant about it?
2. What is significant about the desert?
3. How does Mark describe John the Baptist and his ministry?
4. What is the meaning of Jesus' acceptance of baptism?
5. What events occur at the baptism of Jesus?
6. What influence does the Spirit have on Jesus' ministry?
7. What is significant about the number forty?
8. What does Mark tell us about Jesus' temptation in the desert?

Closing Prayer (SEE PAGE 18)

Pray the closing prayer at this time or after *lectio divina*.

Lectio Divina (SEE PAGE 11)

Relax your body and maintain a posture of prayer (back straight, eyes shut, feet flat on the floor). This exercise can take as long as you want, but in the context of this Bible study, 10 to 20 minutes should be sufficient.

The meditations that follow are provided only to help group participants use this prayer form, but note that *lectio* is intended to bring one to a place of prayerful contemplation where the Word of God speaks to the hearer from his or her heart. (See page 11 for further instruction.)

Jesus Christ, the Son of God (1:1)

As Christians born more than 2,000 years after the birth of Jesus, we could miss the impact of Mark's opening sentence. This is the Good News of Jesus, the Christ, the Son of God. Astounding! We're familiar enough with Jesus' identity as the Son of God that we may take it for granted. Mark's opening line invites us to look at the idea that Jesus is *the Christ*, the Son of God, as though seeing it for the first time.

✠ *What can I learn from this passage?*

The Preaching of John the Baptist (1:2–8)

Readers of Mark's Gospel in the early Church are already aware of the sacrament of baptism, which comes through Christ's resurrection and ascension, as well as the gift of the Holy Spirit, which comes through baptism. When Christians read the Gospel, they understand John the Baptist when he says Jesus will baptize with the Holy Spirit. Paul the apostle stresses the importance of baptism: "For through faith you are all children of God in Christ Jesus. For all of you who were baptized into Christ have clothed yourselves with Christ" (Galatians 3:26–27).

✠ *What can I learn from this passage?*

The Baptism of Jesus (1:9–11)

Maximilian Kolbe was an inmate in a concentration camp. When an inmate with a family was chosen for death, Kolbe offered to suffer and die in his place. Kolbe realized that through his baptism, he was baptized into the death of Jesus. Jesus, who is free of sin, is an example for Kolbe and others who are baptized. He offered himself to die for others. He bears our sins as he commits himself to his mission through his baptism by John.

✠ *What can I learn from this passage?*

The Temptation of Jesus (1:12–13)

If we believe Jesus is the Son of God, we have proof that the Holy Spirit is guiding us. Paul the apostle says "no one can say, 'Jesus is Lord,' except by the holy Spirit" (1 Corinthians 12:3). One of the first acts of the Spirit is not to drive Jesus into a garden of paradise, but to drive him into the desert. Jesus faces his mission by confronting Satan's power. In the desert, as in his life, Jesus lives in the midst of danger. When we were baptized, we weren't immediately lifted out of this life into a warm and luxuriant life of heaven. Like Jesus, the Spirit drives us into the daily struggles of life. We must confront our demons and temptations, overcoming them as Jesus did. The Spirit enables us to live with the belief that God is with us in our struggles, but we must still struggle to live as children of God.

✠ *What can I learn from this passage?*

INDIVIDUAL STUDY

This lesson does not have an Individual Study component.

LESSON 2

The Mystery of Jesus

MARK 1:14–3:6

This is the time of fulfillment. The kingdom of God is at hand. Repent, and believe in the gospel. (1:15)

Opening Prayer (SEE PAGE 18)

Context

Part 1: Mark 1:14–45 Jesus announces that the reign of God has arrived and prepares for the kingdom by preaching, choosing disciples, and healing. He invites Peter, Andrew, James, and John to follow him. He shows that the kingdom has arrived by preaching and healing with authority. The demons he casts out try to shout out his true identity, but Jesus silences them because it's not yet time. Jesus' healing of a man with leprosy inspires large crowds to follow him.

Part 2: Mark 2—3:6 Jesus' forgiveness and healing of a paralyzed man is a later sign that God's reign arrived with the coming of Jesus. When he calls the tax collector Levi to be his disciple, he enters the first of five conflict stories involving forgiveness of sin, eating and drinking with sinners, and answering questions about fasting, working on the Sabbath, and healing on the Sabbath.

PART 1: GROUP STUDY (MARK 1:14–45)

Read Mark 1:14–45 aloud.

1:14–15 The Beginning of Jesus' Galilean Ministry

Herod's arrest of John the Baptist signals the end of John's mission and the beginning of Jesus' ministry. Jesus comes to Galilee in northern Palestine, where he will fulfill most of his public ministry before he is arrested and condemned in Jerusalem. He declares that this is a time of fulfillment when he will bring salvation to the world. Jesus has confronted and overcome Satan in the desert, but his ministry will be one of continual confrontation against evil.

Unlike John the Baptist, who called the people to repentance and confession of sins, Jesus declares that the "kingdom of God is at hand," adding, "Repent and believe in the gospel." Although the gospels use the term *kingdom of God*, we should avoid seeing the kingdom of God as a place. The term actually encompasses a reign over all creation. When Jesus proclaims that the reign of God is "at hand," he declares that God is more active in creation through Jesus. Jesus' proclamation about the reign of God is central to the Gospels of Matthew, Mark, and Luke.

Like John the Baptist, Jesus doesn't simply call people to move away from their sins; he also calls them to move forward. The kingdom of God proclaimed by Jesus becomes present with him and will reach its fulfillment at the end of time. Although Jesus' disciples continue to live in this world, their true goal is to live the gospel by following the example of Jesus' life and message. That's what is meant by the phrase "living in the kingdom of God."

1:16–20 The Call of the First Disciples

Now that Jesus has proclaimed the reign of God to be at hand, he must choose disciples to bring the Good News to the world. As he passes the Sea of Galilee he encounters two fishermen, brothers Andrew and Simon Peter. Jesus promises to make them fishers of human beings, and they immediately leave their nets to follow him. Jesus next calls to James and John, who are in a boat mending their nets. They immediately abandon not only their work, but also their families and hired workers. In writing about these encounters, Mark teaches about discipleship, showing the unwavering, immediate, and total response of true disciples to Jesus' call.

Mark teaches that a disciple isn't one who chooses to follow Jesus, but one who is chosen by Jesus. In Jesus' day, a disciple would approach a religious teacher, but as Jesus tells his disciples in the Gospel of John, "It was not you who chose me, but I who chose you" (15:16).

Christians enduring suffering and death can find encouragement in this message. Knowing that Jesus has chosen them sustains Christians no matter how intense their suffering. Many of the early martyrs in the Church rejoiced when they were chosen to die for Christ. By their life and death, they considered themselves to be preaching a message about Jesus Christ. The author of Mark's Gospel was most likely well aware of the heroism and dedication of these early martyrs.

1:21–28 The Cure of a Man Possessed by Demons

Mark presents Jesus' typical day of teaching, healing, and confronting evil spirits. Jesus comes to Capernaum, which is where he settles during his ministry. On a Sabbath, he enters the synagogue and begins to teach. Perhaps the leaders of the synagogue, in recognition of his education or as a gesture of hospitality, called on him. Jesus astonishes his audience by preaching with the authority of a prophet rather than by quoting scribes and prophets.

Jesus confronts an unclean spirit who addresses him as "Jesus of Nazareth." The demon further identifies Jesus as the "Holy One of God." Many in Jesus' day believed that knowing and using someone's name would give a person power over the one named. Jesus commands the shrieking demon to keep silent and casts it out of the man. This is the first of many instances where we encounter the messianic secret in Mark's Gospel. Because Jesus is more powerful than the evil spirit, it must obey his command. Jesus' power over demons shows that the reign of God has begun.

As the demon leaves the man, the demon's last futile act is to cause the man to have convulsions and cry out. The drama of this event proves to the crowd that the evil spirit has clearly left the man. When Jesus casts out demons throughout the gospel, the person being healed lets out a loud cry, a last shriek from the fleeing demon. The astonished crowd views Jesus' authority and power over the unclean spirit as another form of teaching with authority. In Jesus, a new and more powerful enemy of the unclean spirit has entered the world, giving hope to those under the power of such a spirit. The drama has many subtle characteristics.

According to Jewish Law, a good Jew avoids a possessed person lest he or she also become defiled. Possessed people defile the places they enter; if Jesus didn't perform an exorcism here, the synagogue would be defiled. Mark doesn't tell us how the possessed person was able to enter the synagogue; he simply puts the man in the midst of the assembly. The demon confronts Jesus to identify him and hold power over him, but Jesus is more powerful. Jesus shows the power of good over evil. Anyone who trusts in God and acts accordingly can overcome evil with goodness. To the eyes of the world, those suffering persecution and death seem to be losing, but a large number of witnesses to the early martyrs' heroism became followers of Christ.

Mark portrays the spread of Jesus' fame throughout the region of Galilee, an area far north of Jerusalem. Jesus must become more cautious about being identified as the Messiah, because the Roman authorities have dealt with others who identified themselves as the Messiah to overthrow Roman rule. Anyone identified as the Messiah would be suspected of inciting the people.

1:29–34 Peter's Mother-in-Law and Other Healings

After Jesus leaves the synagogue, he and James and John go to the home of Simon and Andrew and hear that Simon's mother-in-law is in bed with a fever. This short episode tells us that Simon was married and may have had children. Simon's mother-in-law lived with Simon and his family. Simon opens his house to Jesus, symbolically accepting Jesus into his life.

The people of Jesus' era believed that sickness was caused by demons. Jesus' disciples tell Jesus about the fever immediately, perhaps to warn him about the demon. Jesus grasps the woman's hand and the fever leaves her, symbolizing to the people that the evil spirit has left her. The episode tells us that Jesus brings healing not only with his words, but also with his touch. With the enthusiasm of a true disciple, Peter's mother-in-law rises and begins to wait on them. Mark is telling us that the call to discipleship is a call to serve others.

The day ends with a summary of Jesus' ministry. The number of people coming to Jesus may have been large, but Mark exaggerates when he says the whole town gathered. When Jesus casts out demons and orders them not to reveal his identity, they must obey Jesus' command.

1:35–39 Jesus Leaves Capernaum

Early the next morning, Jesus goes off by himself to a deserted place to pray. The disciples rush out to find Jesus, and Mark significantly names Simon and adds "those who were with him" as finding Jesus. They are excited and proud of their relationship with their newfound friend, and they declare excitedly that everyone is looking for him. Jesus realizes that the people and even Simon misunderstand the meaning of his miracles. The miracles aren't publicity stunts; they point to the message he teaches by the manner in which he lives.

Jesus' actions again teach a lesson in discipleship. Discipleship demands periods of prayer that keep Jesus and his disciples focused on their mission as they seek strength and guidance from God. Mark ends the passage with a summary statement about Jesus' preaching in synagogues and casting out demons throughout Galilee. Synagogues, as the centers of worship and learning, were the gathering places for many Jews, and this is the second time Mark mentions that Jesus visited them.

1:40–45 The Cleansing of a Man With Leprosy

The Jewish people of Jesus' day linked a number of unexplained skin diseases with the dreaded disease leprosy. Religious Law forbade a person with leprosy to mix with the community.

A man with leprosy begs Jesus to heal him, saying Jesus could will him clean. Under the Law of Moses, people with leprosy could have no contact with the community until they underwent a ritual purification by the priests, but Jesus responds with compassion by touching the man and healing him. Then he orders the man to show himself to the priests in accord with the Law. This passage shows that Jesus, a good Jew, had respect for the Law of Moses.

Jesus orders the healed man not to tell others about the incident but unlike the demons, who must obey Jesus, the man has free will. He spreads the word of Jesus' miracle, and the crowds following Jesus increase. His rapidly growing popularity forces him to avoid public places and remain in the desert, where the crowds must come to him. By the end of chapter one, Jesus is already well known and acclaimed by the people.

The cleansing of the man with leprosy conveys a message about prayer. Although the man's condition is obvious, he begs Jesus to cleanse him. In recognition of Jesus' exalted position, the man humbly begins his request with "If you wish." The passage provides an insight into prayer, namely the necessity for us to express our needs even though God already knows them. It's also the humble acknowledgement that the type of response depends on God's will.

Review Questions

1. What does Jesus mean when he says the kingdom of God "is at hand"?
2. What is an example of Jesus' use of the messianic secret?
3. What is the message behind Jesus' healing of Simon Peter's mother-in-law?
4. Why is prayer important to Jesus?
5. What lessons does Jesus teach by moving on to other towns to preach instead of remaining with those who recognize his great power?
6. What lesson about prayer can we learn from Jesus' healing of the man with leprosy?
7. What does the early part of the gospel tell us about discipleship?

Closing Prayer (SEE PAGE 18)

Pray the closing prayer now or after *lectio divina*.

Lectio Divina (SEE PAGE 11)

Relax your body and maintain a posture of prayer (back straight, eyes shut, feet flat on the floor). This exercise can take as long as you want, but in the context of this Bible study, 10 to 20 minutes should be sufficient.

The meditations that follow are provided only to help group participants use this prayer form, but note that *lectio* is intended to bring one to a place of prayerful contemplation where the Word of God speaks to the hearer from his or her heart. (See page 11 for further instruction.)

The Beginning of Jesus' Galilean Ministry (1:14–15)

John the Baptist dies, but his message continues through his followers and through the message of Jesus, who brings it to fulfillment. Jesus preached about the reign of God on Earth, a reign of justice, peace, and love. No matter how strong evil appears to be, God is still in control. Jesus calls us to repent and live the Gospel—the Good News of Jesus Christ. We live the Good News when we reflect Christ's presence in the world. Jesus doesn't call us only to repent—he also calls us to live the Good News. We were baptized into Christ, and now we must live in Christ.

✠ *What can I learn from this passage?*

The Call of the First Disciples (1:16–20)

In the year 107, Saint Ignatius of Antioch traveled from Antioch to face death in the arena in Rome because he openly professed faith in Christ. Certain Christians were plotting to free him, but he wrote and told them not to try to save him. He felt it was an honor and a gift to die for Christ. Because he believed Christ chose him, he was prepared to die for Christ.

Jesus has chosen us, and with God's help we will respond with the dedication and courage of the heroic and saintly people of the past. We may not have to suffer or die for our faith, but we face other struggles, especially the struggle to remain faithful to Christ in sinful environments.

✠ *What can I learn from this passage?*

The Cure of a Man Possessed by Demons (1:21–28)

When Jesus confronted the possessed man, the demon tried to overcome Jesus by naming him, but Jesus stood his ground and cast the demon out. The man who would be considered unclean suddenly became the center of attention, forcing those in the synagogue to wonder who Jesus was. We can cast out demons in the world by supporting others who are being ridiculed, rejected, or oppressed unjustly.

✠ *What can I learn from this passage?*

Peter's Mother-in-Law and Other Healings (1:29–34)

Jesus, the Son of God, demands no special treatment. He doesn't visit a castle, but the home of Simon Peter's family. Simon's mother-in-law is in bed with a fever and is too weak to serve them. Fevers in Jesus' era were not as easily treated as they are today and would have been a matter of grave concern for Simon and his family. Jesus relieves the situation by healing her. As a true disciple, Simon's mother-in-law immediately serves others as all disciples are called to do.

✠ *What can I learn from this passage?*

Jesus Leaves Capernaum (1:35–39)

God has a mission for us, but we have to give God time to speak with us each day in prayer. We don't hear God's voice, but we leave prayer with a truer focus on our mission. Jesus rose early in the morning to pray and focus on his mission, which was to share the Word of God—not to stop and enjoy the applause of the crowd. In prayer he found the energy, drive, and focus for his mission and decided he must move on to other villages. Prayer helps us focus on God's will.

✠ *What can I learn from this passage?*

The Cleansing of a Man With Leprosy (1:40–45)

Jesus, moved with pity at the suffering of the man with leprosy, touches him, says "I do will it," and heals him. Paul the apostle tells us Jesus "is the image of the invisible God" (Colossians 1:15). The passage about the man with leprosy teaches us that God has compassion for us as we pray and answers our prayer as he wishes. God, who knows all, may not answer our request as directly as Jesus did the sick man's, but God does respond in some manner each time we pray. God never ignores us. God responds as God wishes and for our good, because God loves us. The leprosy story is not a story just about Jesus' miraculous powers, but about God's care and concern for all people.

✠ *What can I learn from this passage?*

PART 2: INDIVIDUAL STUDY (MARK 2—3:6)

Day 1: The Healing of the Paralyzed Man (2:1–12)

From 2:1 to 3:6, Mark strings together five conflict stories to show religious leaders' growing hostility toward Jesus. Each story is a *pronouncement story*—a story shared in the early Church showing Jesus' ability to discern a situation and reply (pronounce) with wisdom. Each conflict story follows a pattern in which (1) a situation is presented, (2) a protest is registered, and (3) Jesus replies to the protest.

Jesus returns to Capernaum. When people discover he's home, the crowd gets so large that the front door is blocked and a paralyzed man can't get in to see Jesus. In this first conflict story, Mark gives a colorful picture: As Jesus preaches, four men tear open the roof and lower the paralyzed man down to Jesus. When Jesus recognizes the great faith of the five men, he tells the paralyzed man his sins are forgiven. The miracle takes place because of the faith of all five men. It's a community act of faith.

Jesus addresses the paralyzed man as "child," which implies that Jesus as God recognizes the man as a child of God. The word *child* connotes a parental love. Some scribes, knowing that only God can forgive sins, think Jesus' attempt to perform an act belonging to God alone is blasphemy. The theme of blasphemy later becomes a central accusation brought against Jesus at his trial before the Sanhedrin and the motive for declaring that Jesus deserves death (14:60–64). Jesus reads the scribes' minds and asks which is easier—to say to the paralyzed man that his sins are forgiven or to tell him to pick up his mat and go home. Jesus then tells the paralyzed man to pick up his mat and go home, which he does. When the crowd sees that the man is healed, they are astounded.

In Jesus' day, people believed that sickness signified God's displeasure, while health signified God's favor. The physical healing shows that Jesus has indeed performed the divine act of forgiving sins, leaving the crowd to declare that they've never witnessed anything like this.

Mark actually put two stories together in this narrative. He places a story about forgiving sin in the midst of a story about healing a paralyzed man. Note the pattern of this first conflict story, namely (1) the situation of forgiveness is presented, (2) the scribes murmur within themselves in protest, and (3) Jesus rebukes the scribes and heals the paralyzed man.

Jesus refers to himself as the Son of Man. The pronouncement in this story is that the Son of Man (Jesus) has authority on Earth to forgive sins. In Jesus' day, the title Son of Man was often used to refer to oneself; that is, it was used in place of "I." When Mark was writing his gospel, he included the imagery of a "redeeming Son of Man" who brings redemption through his passion, death, and resurrection. Although Jesus may have used "Son of Man" instead of saying "I," Mark implies more by using the term in this passage. He is saying to his readers that Jesus is the Christ and the Son of God.

Three times in the story we read about picking up a mat and walking. This could be Mark's implication of resurrection from sin in the act of forgiveness. "Pick up your mat and walk" could be a message like "Rise up and walk." The mat played an important role in a peasant's life in Jesus' day. Homeless peasants slept on mats, so in a sense the mat was the peasant's home. Jesus' concern isn't just with healing the man, but also with being assured that the man could take his much-needed mat with him.

Lectio Divina

Spend 8 to 10 minutes in silent contemplation of the following passage:

> A man who spent more than thirty years away from the sacrament of reconciliation decided it was time to confess his sins, but he was afraid of the confessor's reaction. The man had committed every sin except murder. One Sunday morning he decided to enter the church building and, as he told it, he "was hooked." He approached a middle-aged confessor. After they finished, the confessor surprised the man by saying, "I want to thank you for coming to me. I'm happy you've confessed after all these years. God has blessed you, and I'm grateful to be part of that blessing." Jesus was a compassionate person who often revealed God's compassion for sinners.
>
> ✠ *What can I learn from this passage?*

Day 2: The Call of Levi (2:13–17)

Mark tells us Jesus again travels alongside the Sea of Galilee. The second conflict story occurs when Jesus calls Levi, a tax collector, to follow him. He identifies Levi as the "son of Alphaeus," which may signify that Alphaeus is known to some members of the early Church. Because tax collectors paid a set fee for the right to collect taxes for Rome and would often overcharge for the sake of making a greater profit, people scorned tax collectors and looked on them as sinners. Jesus calls Levi to follow him in the same manner Jesus called his first disciples and, like the first disciples, Levi follows Jesus immediately.

The scene shifts to a meal at Levi's home. Sharing a common table had great significance in Jesus' time. To share with those viewed as sinners and tax collectors implies that Jesus willingly accepts their manner of life.

This sets the scene for the second conflict story: (1) Jesus eats with those considered sinners and tax collectors, (2) scribes and Pharisees question the disciples about this scandalous situation, and (3) Jesus responds to their objections with another pronouncement.

Jesus declares that those who are well don't need a physician, while those who are sick do. The sinners are in need of spiritual health, and Jesus is a spiritual physician. The Pharisees, depicted as self-righteous in this story, are the ones Jesus didn't come to call, mainly because they've already decided not to listen to Jesus. Sinners, on the other hand, are prepared to listen to Jesus. By eating with tax collectors and sinners, Jesus reverses the idea that we accept the lifestyles of people with whom we share a meal. The sinners and tax collectors share a meal with Jesus, in effect accepting his values and message. Jesus declares that just as the sick and not the well need physicians, Jesus calls sinners—not the self-righteous.

The Pharisees don't complain to Jesus, but to his disciples. Not only does this conflict story teach that Jesus, as the Son of God, seeks out sinners to redeem them, it also shows that in addressing Jesus' disciples, the scribes and Pharisees recognize that Jesus has become a leader. They identify those who follow him as his disciples.

When Mark was composing his gospel, members of the young Christian community found themselves at odds with each other concerning the place of Jewish Law within Christianity. Within the Church, some vehemently wanted Jewish Law and custom preserved and some didn't want to burden converts with Jewish Law. Some went to extremes, like the apostle Paul, whose mission was challenged by Jewish Christians who wanted to preserve Jewish Law. Some on each side viewed the others as sinners.

Mark, however, can point to Jesus' example and the need for Jesus' disciples to have the same attitude toward each other. A true disciple of Jesus' forfeits the right to condemn another. In Jesus' day, not all those who collected taxes for Rome were cheaters, but all were viewed that way.

Lectio Divina

Spend 8 to 10 minutes in silent contemplation of the following passage:

> In the New Testament, meals often imply a connection with the eucharistic meal. During the eucharistic celebration, saints and sinners alike have a right to sit at the table with Jesus. Just as Jesus ate with sinners during his lifetime, he expects to share with sinners in the Eucharist. In reality, when we approach Jesus in Communion, we're not declaring that we are sinless and worthy of the Eucharist—we're admitting that we are weak human beings in need of sharing the Lord's table.

✠ *What can I learn from this passage?*

_____

Day 3: The Question About Fasting (2:18–22)

In the third conflict story, the people come to Jesus to express their concern about his disciples' lack of fasting. The people note that both John the Baptist's and the Pharisees' disciples fast. Pharisees didn't have disciples, so the reference must have been to the Pharisees themselves, who performed weekly fasts. Since John the Baptist was an ascetic who must have fasted often, it isn't surprising that his disciples would too.

In answer to the question about fasting, Jesus declares that wedding guests can't fast while the bridegroom is present, but that when the bridegroom is taken away—as Jesus will be through his death—the disciples will fast.

Mark seems to be explaining to the early Church community why they should fast. The marriage and banquet image is found in the Old Testament to express a nuptial celebration between God and God's people.

Mark and the members of the early Church recognize Jesus' divinity, and therefore view him as the bridegroom. It isn't appropriate to fast while the bridegroom is present; once he leaves, however, it's time to fast. During Jesus' lifetime, the disciples should rejoice and feast in his presence because they're living through the period of the Good News of Jesus Christ. Mark, knowing the end of the story, has Jesus proclaim that once the bridegroom "is taken away"—a reference to his death—the disciples will have reason to fast.

Mark wrote his gospel at a time when Christians were still conflicted about the need to remain faithful to all the directives of the Law of Moses. After Jesus' death his followers fast, but not for the same reason the Pharisees fast. The disciples' fast will take place in union with Jesus the Christ, the Son of God—not to the prescription of the Mosaic Law, but in memory of Jesus Christ.

In the two parables Mark adds to this third conflict story, Jesus states that the new law cannot be made to fit the old law. Like a new patch on an old cloth, it will pull away at the first washing when it shrinks, and the tear will be worse than before. The second parable speaks about new wine in old wineskins. The new wine will break the old wineskins, and the wine will be lost. The new law and reason for fasting fulfills the old, but it can't be made to fit into the old. Many other Jewish customs and traditions won't fit the new way of life flowing from Jesus' message.

Lectio Divina

Spend 8 to 10 minutes in silent contemplation of the following passage:

> A woman at a wedding reception filled her plate with everything she could get on it. When she passed a friend, the friend said, "I thought you were on a diet." The woman answered, "I am, but I wouldn't insult the bride and groom by dieting at a wedding." Jesus uses a similar excuse for his disciples' not fasting. It's now a time for celebrating, but the time for fasting (our time) will come later. The Church today recognizes the value of fasting as a form of penance and prayer. We don't fast for the sake of fasting or to diet, but to be conscious of making a sacrifice for the sake of God.
>
> ✠ *What can I learn from this passage?*

Day 4: The Disciples and the Sabbath (2:23–28)

In the fourth conflict story, the Pharisees complain directly to Jesus when they see his disciples plucking grain on the Sabbath. The Pharisees apparently considered plucking to be equivalent to harvesting, so they judge the disciples to be violating the Sabbath. Jesus responds by alluding to an event in the life of David, who was revered by the Jewish leadership. He had entered the Temple with his army and eaten the Temple bread reserved for the priests (1 Samuel 21:1–7). Because of their need, David and his army were no longer bound by the Mosaic Law, but were actually bound by the higher law of nourishment for his troops. Mark mistakenly identifies Abiathar as high priest during the time of David, while Ahimelech, the father of Abiathar, was actually high priest at the time.

Mark includes two pronouncements in this story. The first—that the Sabbath was made for the sake of human beings, not vice versa—most likely belonged to the story. The second pronouncement, which is placed by Mark, states that the Son of Man (Jesus) is Lord, even of the Sabbath. This last statement emphasizes Jesus' divine authority and reflects the faith of the early Church after Jesus' resurrection. It's unlikely that Jesus would at this point refer to himself by using the image of the Son of Man as a sign of his divinity.

Lectio Divina

Spend 8 to 10 minutes in silent contemplation of the following passage:

> The author of the Book of Genesis tells us, "God blessed the seventh day and made it holy, because on it he rested from all the work he had done in creation" (2:3). The Sabbath was meant to be a day for holiness, a day when human beings rest from their labor and praise God. God gave us the Sabbath rest for the sake of building a relationship between human beings and God, not for the sake of placing numerous burdens on human beings. Jesus, as God, is indeed the Lord of the Sabbath and has the right to correct false interpretations of the Sabbath rest.

✠ *What can I learn from this passage?*

Day 5: A Man With a Withered Hand (3:1–6)

In the fifth and final conflict story, Jesus sets the scene. In a synagogue, Jesus knows his adversaries are watching him closely when he invites a man with a shriveled hand to stand before him. The Pharisees seek to accuse Jesus of breaking the law that forbids healing on the Sabbath unless there is danger of death. Jesus has already challenged the Pharisees about their strict interpretations of Sabbath observance. They're seething over past conflicts with Jesus, and they're anxious to trap Jesus in an act of violating the Sabbath.

Jesus asks whether a person may perform a good deed on the Sabbath if not performing it would be evil. Since the Pharisees can't admit that refusing to cure a person on the Sabbath is indeed an evil act without contradicting their strict rules and condemning themselves, they remain silent. Jesus gets angry and grieves their refusal to answer him. His intent isn't to make fools of them, but to educate them about God's attitude toward Sabbath Law.

Jesus heals the withered hand. The shadow of the cross again falls over the narrative as an unlikely alliance forms between the Pharisees and Herod's followers, and they begin to plot Jesus' death. The religious leaders can condemn someone, but they don't have the authority to carry out the order. Only civil authorities can command someone's death. The Pharisees and Herod's followers are working together to carry out Jesus' death sentence.

Lectio Divina

Spend 8 to 10 minutes in silent contemplation of the following passage:

This Scripture passage speaks of mercy while condemning a rigidity that ignores the needs of the health of human beings. Like many other passages in Scripture, the law of love of God and neighbor supersedes every rigid interpretation of the Law. The Lord's Day is a day for doing good, not evil. It's a day for saving life, not destroying it. Jesus was angry and grieved that religious leaders distorted the meaning of the Sabbath.

✠ *What can I learn from this passage?*

Review Questions

1. Why is it important for Jesus to heal the paralyzed man?
2. Why do the scribes see Jesus as blaspheming when he claims to forgive sins?
3. Why do the Pharisees get upset when Jesus eats with tax collectors and sinners? How does Jesus respond to their reaction?
4. Who is Levi?
5. What is the significance of the Pharisees' complaint to Jesus' disciples?
6. What reason does Jesus give for his disciples' not fasting?
7. What is the meaning of Jesus' parables about a new patch on an old cloth and new wine in old wineskins?
8. What is the problem with plucking grain on the Sabbath, and how does Jesus respond to the complaint?
9. Why does conflict arise when Jesus heals the man with the withered hand on the Sabbath?
10. What is the significance of the Pharisees' and Herodians' plans for Jesus' death?

The Mystery of the Reign of God

MARK 3:7—5

He woke up, rebuked the wind, and said to the sea, "Quiet! Be still!" The wind ceased and there was great calm. Then he asked them, "Why are you terrified? Do you not yet have faith?" (4:39–40)

Opening Prayer (SEE PAGE 18)

Context

Note: *In this lesson, Part 1 takes place scripturally after Part 2 because the passages in Part 1 are more appropriate for group study.*

Part 1: Mark 4:35—5 Four of Jesus' miracles follow Jesus' parables: Jesus walks on water, heals a man possessed by demons, raises the deceased daughter of a synagogue official, and heals a woman who had been hemorrhaging for twelve years. Like the parables, the miracles are instructions to prepare Jesus' disciples for ministry.

Part 2: Mark 3:7—4:34 Jesus chooses twelve apostles, whom he sends out to preach and gives the authority to cast out demons. He returns home and debates some scribes who accuse him of casting out demons by the power of the king of demons. Jesus reduces their accusation to its absurd conclusion, saying that a kingdom (of evil) divided against itself cannot stand. Jesus is performing good actions, not evil ones. Later, he tells a parable: The reign of God is like a seed sown in a field that produces good and bad fruit. It's up to the receiver to accept Jesus' words. The reign of God becomes central in Jesus' ministry as he chooses the Twelve for his mission, defends himself against foolish accusations, and teaches about the reign of God.

PART 1: GROUP STUDY (MARK 4:35—5)

Read Mark 4:35—5 aloud.

4:35–41 Jesus Calms the Seas

As a transition from his day with the crowd and as evening approaches, a weary Jesus urges his disciples to cross to the other side of the sea. Other boats accompany them, showing the crowd's persistence in following Jesus. The crossing signals a change in Mark's Gospel as Mark moves from Jesus' parables to Jesus' miracles.

In the midst of the journey, Jesus is comfortably sleeping on a cushion when a violent squall sends waves crashing over the boat and threatens to sink the vessel. The sleep symbolizes trust in God. Sudden storms often rose with little warning on the Sea of Galilee. The disciples, in a panic and fearful that they will drown, awaken Jesus to warn him of the danger. In Mark's Gospel the disciples refer to Jesus at this point as "teacher," show-ing that they haven't yet come to faith in Jesus as the Christ. They don't ask Jesus to help them; they simply alert him to the danger.

In Jesus' day, people believed that evil spirits dwelt in the sea and that the swelling seas arose as when those spirits were agitated. Ability to calm the seas would be a sign of power over evil spirits and of the divine power that belongs only to God. Mark doesn't tell us Jesus calms the sea—he says Jesus "rebuked the wind," as though he is rebuking evil spirits, and he sternly commands the sea, "Quiet! Be still!" This command is similar to that found earlier in Mark's Gospel, when Jesus casts an evil spirit out of a man with the command, "Quiet! Come out of him!" (1:25). The wind ceases, and great calm follows. Jesus rebukes his disciples for their lack of faith. The disciples, however, have a new lesson to ponder: Who is this man that even the wind and sea obey him?

5:1–20 The Healing of a Man Who Was Possessed

After the storm, the boat lands on the other side of the sea in the Gentile territory of Gerasene. A strong and shrieking possessed man rushes toward Jesus from the tombs, the place where the people believe demons dwell. The possessed man, who couldn't be restrained with chains, rushes to Jesus. The demons possessing him can't control themselves, paying homage to Jesus while frantically asking what Jesus has to do with him. The demons identify Jesus as the Son of God Most High. Jesus forces the demons to identify themselves, and their name—"Legion"—indicates that many demons possess the man. They beg Jesus to send them into some nearby swine instead of casting them out of the land. Swine were considered unclean animals and certainly worthy of the demons' presence. The demons didn't wish Jesus to cast them out of the land, but when he casts them into the swine they panic and charge off a cliff, casting themselves out of the land. The swine's rush off the cliff attests to the number of demons as well as their lack of control in Jesus' presence.

The swine herders spread word of the incident. When people come to see what transpired, they find the possessed man completely subdued and calm. Fearing that Jesus is a stronger demon, they beg him to leave their territory. As he leaves, Jesus tells the formerly possessed man to go home, thus giving the man and his family a compassionate gift they've most likely not enjoyed for years. Jesus also tells the man to spread word of the miracle, which seems to contradict the messianic secret; however, Jesus was in Gentile territory, where the people didn't have false notions or ideas about a Messiah. The formerly possessed man becomes an evangelist, proclaiming what Jesus did for him.

When Mark wrote his gospel, many Gentiles had already professed their faith in Jesus as the Christ and the Son of God. Mark stresses here that by curing the man and telling him to spread news of the miracle to others, Jesus sought converts from among the Gentiles.

5:21–43 Jairus's Daughter and the Woman With a Hemorrhage

Jesus again crosses to the other side of the sea, and Mark presents two miracle stories in one long passage. The theme of both stories is the power of faith. An official of the synagogue, Jairus, begs Jesus to heal his critically ill little daughter. Along the way, a woman of faith who has been hemorrhaging for many years touches Jesus' cloak and is healed. That Jesus doesn't directly cause the healing by willing it shows the power of faith in the healing. Jesus feels power going out from him, as though the woman's faith is drawing it from him. When she confesses that she touched him, Jesus commends her for her faith. The disciples, who tried to tell Jesus it was foolish to ask who touched him in the midst of the large crowd, are portrayed as men with lesser faith.

When messengers arrive to tell Jesus and the synagogue official that the little girl is dead, Jesus urges the official to have faith. Jesus takes three disciples—Peter, James, and John—with him on this journey as he does on other significant journeys such as the transfiguration (9:2–8) and the agony in the garden (14:32–42). When Mark tells us Jesus chooses Peter, James, and John to be with him, we're warned that something significant is about to happen. They arrive at the house to find that the mourners have already arrived, which proves the girl has truly died.

In the early Church, belief in the resurrection and the second coming of Christ led people to speak of the dead as being asleep. In the same way, Jesus proclaims the child is asleep. Since the mourners lack the necessary faith for this miracle, Jesus asks them to leave. He then takes the girl by the hand and orders her to rise. For the people of Jesus' time, the ability to eat was a sign that someone was truly alive. Jesus tells the parents to give the child something to eat. Now that he's back in Palestine, Jesus urges them not to tell anyone what has taken place. Mark continues to make use of the messianic secret.

Jesus' touch plays an important role in the stories of Jairus's deceased daughter and the woman with hemorrhages. Laying hands on a person is seldom found in Jewish stories of healing, but it occurs at least five times in Mark's Gospel. Mark also repeats the idea that a person may be healed by touching Jesus or his garment. The woman with the hemorrhages touches

Jesus' cloak, and the young girl is raised when Jesus takes her by the hand and tells her to rise. The faith of Jairus and the woman who touched Jesus' cloak is central to the stories.

Mark uses the literary technique of placing one story between another; he does this in several places in his gospel. The stories are linked because they are stories of faith in action. They also offer insight into Jesus, the image of the invisible God. Jairus doesn't hesitate to approach Jesus, who immediately responds. Jesus, the Son of God, is approachable and available. He is compassionate and shows a true reflection of God's love for all people.

Review Questions

1. What message about faith do we get from the story of Jesus asleep in the boat?
2. What is significant about Jesus' calming the storm?
3. What message about faith do we get from the story of the possessed man?
4. What does the story of the possessed man reveal about the demons' attitude when they're in Jesus' presence?
5. Why do the people of Gerasene want Jesus to leave their territory?
6. What message about faith do we get from the story of Jairus's daughter and the woman with the hemorrhage?

Closing Prayer (SEE PAGE 18)

Pray the closing prayer now or after *lectio divina*.

Lectio Divina (SEE PAGE 11)

Relax your body and maintain a posture of prayer (back straight, eyes shut, feet flat on the floor). This exercise can take as long as you want, but in the context of this Bible study, 10 to 20 minutes should be sufficient.

The meditations that follow are provided only to help group participants use this prayer form, but note that *lectio* is intended to bring one to a place of prayerful contemplation where the Word of God speaks to the hearer from his or her heart. (See page 11 for further instruction.)

Jesus Calms the Seas (4:35–41)

Since Mark is writing for Jesus' persecuted followers, he delivers a message of encouragement: Although Jesus appears to be asleep in the midst of the storm, he is awake and with them. He has power over the storms of their lives and will save them or give them strength. We all pray when we have storms in our lives, but at times Jesus seems to be comfortably asleep and uncaring. The reality is just the opposite. Jesus asks us not to be terrified in our life storms because he has power over the demons that haunt us. If we let him, at some point Jesus will calm the storms.

✠ *What can I learn from this passage?*

The Healing of a Man Who Was Possessed (5:1–20)

In 1935 Bill W. and Dr. Bob, two men struggling to overcome the destruction alcohol was causing in their lives, began Alcoholics Anonymous. Their twelve steps for sobriety include admission of weakness, trust in a divine being, and prayer to that divine being. In the years since, millions of men and women have controlled their addiction demons with the help of AA. Although a spiritual exorcism didn't occur, a true casting out of demons has taken place for these recovering alcoholics. This is only one example of the demons we encounter. Physical, emotional, and spiritual demons are legion and sometimes seem impossible to destroy. Through prayer and trust in God, however, many are controlling their demons.

✠ *What can I learn from this passage?*

Jairus's Daughter and the Woman With a Hemorrhage (5:21–43)

Mark continually emphasizes the importance of strong faith. Faith and touch play an important role in the stories of Jairus's daughter and the woman with the hemorrhage. We are able to touch Jesus in our prayers not physically, but spiritually. Friends who won't see each other for a while say, "We must keep in touch." Jesus' disciples must always keep in touch with him, recognizing that he is our constant companion.

✠ *What can I learn from this passage?*

PART 2: INDIVIDUAL STUDY (MARK 3:7—4:34)

Day 1: Establishing a Community (3:7–19)

Jesus withdraws toward the sea with his disciples. The crowds who come to Jesus consist of Jews and Gentiles, and Mark lists the many territories they come from to show how far Jesus' fame has spread. Jesus travels from the synagogue to the sea, as though he's moving away from the old Israel to the new. Mark adds a human touch to the story as he mentions Jesus' direction to have a boat ready to keep the rapidly increasing crowd from crushing him. The large size of the crowd increases the religious leaders' hostility toward Jesus. Later they will be afraid of starting a riot if they capture Jesus in public.

Because Jesus was healing so many people, the crowds were pressing in on him, trying to touch him. The unclean spirits possessing some in the crowd fell down before him and screeched, "You are the Son of God." Jesus commanded them harshly not to reveal his identity. The number of people following Jesus, witnessing his miracles, and listening to his words sets the stage for the new people of Israel. Jesus is establishing a community to carry on his ministry after his resurrection and ascension.

Jesus goes up a mountain and summons those he wants to follow him. Mountains have special significance in Scripture. In the Old Testament, God spoke to Moses and certain prophets on a mountain. God visits people on a mountain, a place closer to God. Mountains are where Jesus shares significant messages or makes significant decisions. In this passage, Jesus is about to choose the twelve apostles. The Twelve don't make the choice on their own—Jesus chooses them, and they follow. They are to take part in his mission and be sent out to preach and cast out demons.

The word *apostle* means "one who is sent," whereas a disciple is one who learns. The apostles still have much to learn from Jesus, but Jesus chooses them to share his message. The gospels list twelve apostles, but Paul will later declare that he too is a chosen apostle. He writes, "Paul, an apostle, not from human beings nor through a human being but through Jesus Christ and God the Father who raised him from the dead" (Galatians 1:1).

At this point in Mark's Gospel, Simon receives the name of Peter. In the lists of the Twelve in the other gospels, Peter is always first. The other members of the Twelve include "James, son of Zebedee, and John the brother of James, whom [Jesus] named Boanerges, that is, sons of thunder; Andrew, Philip, Bartholomew, Matthew, Thomas, James the son of Alphaeus; Thaddeus, Simon the Cananean, and Judas Iscariot who betrayed him" (3:16–17). The name Judas Iscariot is always mentioned as the one "who betrayed him."

The number twelve was significant to the people of ancient Israel because it signified the twelve sons of Jacob, whose tribes represented the "chosen people" of the Old Testament. In setting up the New Israel, Jesus now appoints twelve companions who will be known in the early Church as the "Twelve," with a capital T. Although Jesus had many disciples, these twelve will be there to learn from him and become leaders of the "new way" after his ascension.

Lectio Divina

Spend 8 to 10 minutes in silent contemplation of the following passage:

The symbolic images in this passage point to the establishment of a new community. Theologians debate whether Jesus intended to establish a Church. Whether he did or not, he certainly left behind a community that could become the foundation for a new Church community. He chose his disciples to continue to share his message. Today Jesus continues to choose his disciples. As people of faith, we too are disciples of Jesus, chosen by him to be his followers.

✠ *What can I learn from this passage?*

Day 2: Blasphemy of the Scribes (3:20–35)

Jesus' relatives, like the people of his hometown, knew him as a child and refuse to believe he's the person everyone is raving about. They may have heard about his miracles, but they didn't witness them. Believing he has gone out of his mind, they come to seize him. The cost of being a Christian at the time Mark wrote his gospel was very high. Mark is speaking to those of his own era whose families rejected them or thought they were mad for becoming Christian.

Some scribes from Jerusalem, the place of official Judaism, arrive and claim that Jesus is expelling demons under the power of a greater demon known as *Beelzebul*. The allusion is to a false god, Beelzebul, whose name is spelled differently in the Old Testament. In one passage, the king of Samaria seeks the help of *Baalzebub*, a false god, but Elijah tells the king he will die because of this request. He warns, "Is it because there is no God in Israel that you are going to inquire of Baalzebub?" (2 Kings 1:3). The king showed more faith in the false god than he did in the God of Israel. The scribes try to convince the crowd that this prince of demons has possessed Jesus.

Jesus takes control by summoning the scribes and refuting their accusations with two short parables. He doesn't shy away from the debate—he's willing to confront the scribes in front of the crowd. He points out how ridiculous it is to think that Satan would cast out Satan. A kingdom or house divided against itself cannot stand. Logically, if Satan is fighting against himself, his kingdom won't stand. The only reason Jesus can plunder the kingdom of Satan is because he has bound Satan and is therefore stronger than Satan.

In the gospels, Jesus begins significant statements with the expression "Amen, I say to you." Here he emphasizes the message that sins and blasphemies can be forgiven, but those who blaspheme against the Holy Spirit will never be forgiven. This is the unforgivable sin.

Jesus knows that, despite what he says, a number of religious leaders won't listen. They've closed their minds. As Jesus speaks, they're thinking of how to refute him. The people trust these leaders, believing they're the chosen interpreters of the Law, but Jesus' wisdom is making fools of them. Those who reject Jesus' message choose to reject the Holy Spirit's message.

Because the scribes believe Jesus is possessed and have closed their minds to his message, they choose the unforgivable sin and blaspheme against the Holy Spirit. With the grace of God, some could later be open to Jesus' words and accept them. God will forgive them because they're no longer blocking God's message. This Scripture passage reminds us that forgiveness depends on God and the person who receives forgiveness.

The episode began with Jesus' relatives seeking to seize him, and now Jesus' mother and "brothers" arrive and are calling for him. In Jesus' culture, people often referred to a relative who wasn't a brother or sister as a brother or sister. On this occasion, Mark quotes another pronouncement from Jesus: "For whoever does the will of God is my brother and sister and mother" (3:35). Jesus isn't rejecting his family in this passage; he's using the family image to show how important those who do his will are to God.

This is one of two times in Mark's Gospel where Jesus' mother is mentioned with no reference to Joseph or the word *father*. This leads some commentators to conclude that at this point, Joseph had died.

Mark begins this passage with Jesus' relatives being present, then he speaks of the scribes' accusing Jesus of being a demon, and at the end he returns to talking about Jesus' family. In this way, Mark has sandwiched the story about Beelzebul between the stories of Jesus' family, a literary technique used several times in Mark.

Jesus' relatives stood "outside," an image Mark could be using to show that, unlike the believing crowd surrounding Jesus, they don't yet believe in him. Most Christians would be shocked at the idea of Jesus' mother thinking he was mad. This second reference to Jesus' family doesn't say they believe he's out of his mind, although that could be the inference in the context of the total episode.

Lectio Divina

Spend 8 to 10 minutes in silent contemplation of the following passage:

Many good people are accused of being evil because others don't understand them. It happens between countries, between religions, between political parties, between races, and between family members. Jesus had a solution for this when he called us to love God, neighbor, and self, but it's a solution many reject. As good as Jesus was, the scribes who couldn't or didn't wish to understand him rejected him as evil. This story warns us to be cautious in identifying others as evil. The accuser may be the evil one in that circumstance.

✠ *What can I learn from this passage?*

Day 3: The Parable of the Sower (4:1–20)

As Jesus teaches by the sea, the crowd gets so large that Jesus must teach them from a boat. Mark mentions that the crowd was on land. The image of a boat was often used in the early Church as an image of the Church, meaning the Body of Christ on Earth. Mark offers the subtle message that the Church teaches Jesus' message. Jesus sits as he teaches. Sitting is a sign of authority.

Mark introduces a series of Jesus' parables about the reign of God. A parable has one point, whereas an allegory usually has more than one point, each of which teaches a lesson. The first parable is a perfect example of a parable that became an allegory. Jesus speaks of a sower who spreads his seed in a field. In Jesus' day, the sower threw the seed randomly in the field and allowed it to take root wherever it landed. Jesus speaks of the seed falling where it yielded nothing: on the footpath, the rocks, and among thorns. But then, Jesus tells us, seed fell on good soil and yielded an astounding harvest of thirty-, sixty-, and a hundredfold. In Jesus' day, such a large yield would be miraculous. The crowd must have smiled or laughed at this ridiculous conclusion. At the end of the parable, Jesus invites those with ears to hear—that is, he calls those with faith to understand his message.

In a private discussion with the Twelve, Jesus says that the mystery of the kingdom of God is granted to them because of their faith, but he uses parables so that those without faith won't understand. Jesus borrows a portion of his message from Isaiah the prophet, who was sent by God to warn the people of impending doom, but God will "dull their ears and close their eyes" (Isaiah 6:10) because of their unbelief, and they won't understand. In the same manner, Jesus speaks of those who will look, see, hear, and listen, yet not understand because of their lack of faith.

Jesus' parables become clear to those reading Mark's Gospel with faith, because they accept Jesus' words and haven't closed their minds to his message. Mark seems to be saying that God intentionally blocks those without faith from understanding God's message. However, he is actually stating that God allows them to hear, but their closed minds refuse to understand. Our understanding of Jesus' message depends on our openness to hearing what Jesus has to say without letting our personal opinions block the message.

Many commentators believe that the early Church shaped this parable into an allegory by giving meaning to each part of the story. Others, however, believe that allegories were found in ancient Jewish writings and that Jesus' story was actually an allegory from the beginning. But whether Jesus presented it as an allegory or the members of the early Church—under the influence of the Holy Spirit—told it as an allegory, we accept the message as inspired.

Jesus explains the parable as though it is an allegory. He tells his disciples that the seed is the Word of God. He leaves us to identify where we are in the story. The seed that lands on the path represents people who hear the Word of God, but like the birds, Satan snatches it. These people hear the Word but do nothing with it.

The seed that falls on rocky ground represents those who accept the Word with joy, but the Word doesn't take root. They may profess faith in Christ but show no signs of this faith in dealing with others. At the first sign of misfortune or persecution, they fall away.

The seed that falls among the thorns represents people who accept God's Word but let worldly cares choke it out of their lives.

The seed that falls on rich soil represents people who hear the Word of God *and* make it central to their lives. They produce an abundant harvest. Depending on the depth of their faith, they produce a harvest of thirty-, sixty-, or a hundredfold.

The parable as allegory helps readers place themselves in one of the categories: the abundant harvest, the harvest that lacks roots, or the harvest choked by worldly cares. The seed is the Word of God, but we are the soil. How we receive the Word of God is up to us.

Lectio Divina

Spend 8 to 10 minutes in silent contemplation of the following passage:

The parable of the sower speaks of the manner in which different people receive the Word of God, but it can also refer to our reception of the Word of God at different times in our lives. During one period, we may hear the Word of God but refuse to act on it. Another time, we may receive the Word with enthusiasm, but it has no roots and we go off in other directions and forget its importance. Sometimes we receive the Word of God with a sincere desire to learn more about it, but soon we find ourselves too busy or too bound to the cares of everyday life to give time to learning about it. Finally, we may reach a stage where we sincerely want to learn about God's Word, and we devote time to learning and praying with the Word of God. Depending on the time, prayer, and attention we give it, we can produce fruit thirty-, sixty-, or a hundredfold. The Word of God is God speaking to us.

✠ *What can I learn from this passage?*

Day 4: Parable of the Lamp (4:21–25)

Mark links passages from Jesus' wisdom sayings with parable teachings. In their original context, these wise sayings were apparently preached in groups of two and most likely had nothing to do with the parables, but Mark added them to each parable.

Mark adds the first pair of wise sayings to Jesus' parable about a lamp that is brought in to give light, not be hidden under a bushel basket. After this parable, Mark adds Jesus' wise saying that nothing is hidden except to be made visible, and whatever is secret comes to light. Jesus' disciples must understand the light (Jesus) before they can share it. This pair of sayings teaches that the revelations Jesus instills in the Twelve are to be seen by all. The true disciple doesn't hide the light of faith received from Christ.

Mark uses Jesus' call for us to listen with ears of faith as a way of linking the first parable and pair of wise sayings with the pair of parables that follow. Listening with "ears to hear" simply means willingness to listen with the ears of faith.

The second parable initially teaches that the special measure we give the message is the measure we receive. "Measure" (4:24) refers to faith and understanding. The extent of one's faith will lead a person to a greater understanding of the message. The second set of sayings following the parable speaks to those who are open to the parables and those who are not. Those who have (who are open) will receive an even greater gift, while those who have not (who are closed-minded) will lose what they have. Jesus is telling his disciples that to the degree they live by faith, their faith and understanding will grow. But if they don't live by faith, they will eventually lose what faith they had.

Faith doesn't stand still—it either increases through our prayers and actions or decreases if we never let it direct our lives.

Lectio Divina

Spend 8 to 10 minutes in silent contemplation of the following passage:

With our ears of faith, we hear Jesus speaking through the Scriptures. Jesus' words come to us in a revealed concealed way: We wish to know God's will, but we must always wonder if we're truly following God's will for us at every moment. God's will is that we live as well as we can and that we fulfill our obligations as well as we can. In daily life, we are meant to reflect Christ. That is God's will for us, no matter what our profession. Whether we're a laborer, an office worker, a teacher, a janitor, a religious, a homemaker—we have the call to live as a true reflection of Christ in the best way. We are the light of Christ in the world.

✠ *What can I learn from this passage?*

Day 5: Seed Grows of Itself (4:26–29)

Mark presents two more parables that continue to use the theme of planting a seed. The kingdom of God is like a seed that is sown and left to grow on its own. Once the farmer has sown the seed, God provides the growth. When the seed yields a great harvest, the farmer goes to work with his sickle. Harvest time is the day of judgment. The parable could have been chosen by Mark to encourage the early Church community not to grow discouraged over its apparent lack of growth. The full harvest is up to God. Meanwhile, the early community must continue to plant the Word in the world.

Every gift from God begins small, including the gift of faith. We cannot force the growth of our faith, but like the farmer who waters and fertilizes the land, we can nourish our faith through our prayers and actions. God provides the growth in God's good time. Just as the kingdom of God depends on God to give it growth, we depend on God to increase our faith.

Lectio Divina

Spend 8 to 10 minutes in silent contemplation of the following passage:

A strongly anticlerical man named Peregrine became so enraged at a talk given by a saintly cleric named Philip Benizi that he slapped Philip's face. Philip surprised Peregrine by immediately forgiving him and turning the other cheek. *The seed was planted.* Peregrine was so embarrassed by his outrageous action that he apologized to Philip and went off to spend a long time in prayer. *The seed was being nourished.* As penance for his insult to Philip, Peregrine chose to stand whenever he didn't have to sit. He stood for thirty years, causing such painful sores on his leg that doctors decided to amputate it. The night before the surgery, Peregrine prayed for many hours at the foot of a crucifix. Later, he dreamt that Christ touched his foot. In the morning, his leg was completely healed. Peregrine became the patron saint of people with cancer. *The plant grew to harvest.* We pray, and God nourishes us each day until we become the person God wants us to be.

✠ *What can I learn from this passage?*

Day 6: The Mustard Seed (4:30–34)

Jesus delivers a parable about a mustard seed. This is a tiny seed that produces a large bush that provides shade for birds. Jesus applies the parable of the mustard seed to the growth of the reign of God. This parable, like the story of the seed that grows into a harvest in God's good time, is also a parable of encouragement for the early community. From tiny and humble beginnings comes the kingdom of God, which will bring us protection and nourishment.

Jesus continued to speak in parables because the full message of his mission couldn't be understood. He did, however, privately explain the parables' meaning to the disciples. Jesus the teacher is preparing his disciples for their mission by instructing them about the reign of God on a deeper level.

The tiny seed planted on the cross in Jerusalem 2,000 years ago has blossomed into Christianity, which has spread its branches throughout the world, offering spiritual and physical help and protection to countless people. Jesus was unknown to most of the world when he died, but that tiny seed is now known and celebrated as a savior of all people.

This parable was a message of encouragement to a handful of people who had been given an enormous mission. Only with God's help could such a humble and apparently hopeless beginning be fulfilled as Jesus promised.

Lectio Divina

Spend 8 to 10 minutes in silent contemplation of the following passage:

In all these stories, Jesus speaks about seeds being planted. Each Christian's mission is to plant seeds, not to transplant trees. We plant a number of seeds in others' lives, and with God's help the good seeds we sow will become a blossoming tree of life. From a tiny seed in Palestine came a world-changing event. The sower went out to sow his seed, and look what happened.

✠ *What can I learn from these four parables?*

Review Questions

1. Why do so many people follow Jesus?

2. Why do we refer to the apostles as "the Twelve," and what is their mission?

3. Why does Jesus' family think he's out of his mind?

4. How does Jesus confront the accusation that he performs his miracles through the power of Beelzebul?

5. Whom does Jesus identify as his mother, sisters, and brothers?

6. Why does Jesus use parables to teach about the kingdom of God?

7. What is the message of the sower?

8. What is the difference between an allegory and a parable?

9. What are the wise sayings of Jesus concerning the sharing of his message?

10. What is the message behind the seed that was allowed to grow in its own good time?

11. What is the message of the mustard seed?

12. What is the meaning behind the parable of the lamp?

The Power of Faith

MARK 6—8:26

Then, taking the five loaves and the two fish and looking up to heaven, he said the blessing, broke the loaves, and gave them to [his] disciples to set before the people; he also divided the two fish among them all. They all ate and were satisfied. (6:41–42)

Opening Prayer (SEE PAGE 18)

Context

Part 1: Mark 6 Jesus returns to his hometown of Nazareth, where he is unable to perform miracles due to the people's lack of faith. As he moves on to other villages, he urges the Twelve to travel with as little as possible, as though they were on an urgent mission. In the meantime Herod, who'd had John killed, believes Jesus is John the Baptist raised from the dead. When the excited Twelve return from their successful mission, they're unable to rest due to the vast crowd following Jesus. Later, Jesus feeds the crowd with five loaves and two fish in a manner similar to the celebration of the Eucharist. That evening as Jesus' disciples cross the sea against a headwind, they're frightened when Jesus walks on the water. Jesus calms their fears. Back on land, Jesus continues his healing ministry among the people of Gennesaret.

Part 2: Mark 7—8:26 Jesus rebukes the religious leaders for replacing God's laws with human laws. As Jesus travels in Galilee, he heals the daughter of a woman who is not a Jew, showing that Jesus came for all people. He also heals a deaf man with a speech impediment, implying that Jesus brought the gift of hearing and speaking God's Word to people. Jesus miraculously feeds 4,000 people in the desert in a manner similar to his feeding of 5,000 in an earlier story. Later he warns his disciples not to allow the Pharisees to influence them as leaven in dough, but they misunderstand him. And in the final story of this passage, Jesus heals a blind man, who gradually regains his sight. Mark is teaching that the disciples will slowly and gradually recognize Jesus' identity.

PART 1: GROUP STUDY (MARK 6)

Read aloud Mark 6.

6:1–6 Jesus' Rejection at Nazareth

Jesus returns to his hometown of Nazareth and teaches in the synagogue on a Sabbath. The astounded townspeople ask where he gained all this wisdom, and they marvel at his great deeds. Their astonishment, however, turns to skepticism as they recall Jesus' origins, which seem no different from their own. He was a laborer, a carpenter; Mary is his mother.

The people of Jesus' time would ordinarily identify a son in relation to his father rather than to his mother. That they name Jesus as the son of Mary could mean Mary was a widow by that time. They also claim to know his "brothers." A custom of the day was to identify cousins as one's brothers and sisters. When the people identify James, Joseph, Judas, and Simon as Jesus' brothers, they could actually be referring to his cousins. In a later chapter, Mark identifies two of those named as brothers (James and Joseph) as having a different mother (15:40). Because Jesus seems so ordinary, the people of his hometown are unable to recognize who he is. Jesus responds that prophets are often not honored in their native place and among their own kinsmen.

Jesus is distressed at the lack of faith of the people of Nazareth and is unable to work miracles there except for a few incidents of curing the sick. In contrast to Jairus and the woman with the hemorrhage, the people of Jesus' hometown lacked faith. This passage demonstrates that Jesus' miracles were performed in response to the people's faith. It's also a message for followers of Christ—then and now. Unless we act and pray with faith, God can do nothing in our lives. Mark stresses the need for faith in Christ.

6:7–13 Mission of the Twelve

Jesus travels to the villages preaching, and he calls the Twelve to share in his mission. Since the disciples haven't fully grasped Jesus' message, he sends them on a mission similar to John the Baptist's. They don't preach about the kingdom of God but, like the Baptist, they preach about the need for repentance.

Jesus gives the Twelve power over unclean spirits and sends them out in pairs, which was the custom of missionary travel. They are to travel as poor preachers, taking nothing with them except a walking stick. They are to depend on the generosity of those they preach to. Taking little or nothing with them underlines the urgency of their mission. Rather than moving from one house to another, they are to stay at the first house they're welcomed to. This will keep them focused on their mission instead of on seeking better accommodations. If anyone rejects them, the Twelve are to follow the custom of brushing the dust of that town from their feet as a witness before God against that town. The Twelve expel demons, anoint the sick with oil, and cure many. Oil was used for physical healing; the Twelve use oil for spiritual healing.

The mission of the Twelve reflects the mission of Jesus who, at the beginning of the Gospel of Mark, moved from village to village preaching his message. He returned occasionally to his home in Capernaum, but even there large crowds came to him. Jesus' movements, like those of his disciples, demonstrate the urgency of the mission.

6:14–29 Death of John the Baptist

The gospels identify John the Baptist with the Old Testament figure Elijah the prophet. People believed Elijah would return before the coming of the day of the Lord (Malachi 3:22–24; in some versions of the Bible, this verse is numbered 4:5). When King Herod (c. 4 BC–AD 39) hears about Jesus, he fears Jesus might be John the Baptist raised from the dead. Others think Jesus may be Elijah, while still others think he's like the prophets of the past.

Certain elements of John the Baptist's death reflect the incidents surrounding the prophet Elijah in the Old Testament (1 Kings 19:1–3; 21). Jezebel, wife of King Ahab, forces Elijah to flee for his life. Herod's wife, Herodias, becomes the new Jezebel in the narrative about the Baptist's death. Mark relates how the Baptist accused Herod of sinning by marrying his brother Philip's wife. This wasn't true; Herodias's first husband was a different Herod, Herod Antipas's half-brother.

The story of Salome's dance reflects episodes from the Old Testament story of Esther. Esther pleased the king, and he told her she could have whatever she wanted, even half of his kingdom (5:3–8). Like Jezebel in the Old Testament, Herodias seeks the life of a prophet and takes advantage of the king's foolish promise. Herodias, through her daughter, asks for the head of John the Baptist. Despite his reluctance, Herod has John's head brought in on a platter.

In his guilt, Herod believes that Jesus is actually John the Baptist raised from the dead. Although Herod ordinarily had no problem beheading someone, he was superstitious, as many people were in that era. He would consider the resurrection of John the Baptist a threat to his own existence. No one wanted to fight ghosts or someone who was once dead and is now alive.

The narrative of John the Baptist's death foreshadows the death of Jesus, who will also will be put to death by a Roman ruler. When Jesus dies, his disciples—like John the Baptist's—will take his body and lay it in a tomb. Even in death, John the Baptist prepares the way of the Lord.

6:30–44 Feeding 5,000 in the Desert

Mark returns to the story that introduced this episode. The excited apostles return with news of their activities. Mark significantly identifies them as *apostles,* as though the mission gives them a new identity. Jesus invites them off to a place in the desert that is apart from the crowds but is apparently known to their followers, because people have arrived ahead of them. This sets the scene for the next episode: the multiplication of the loaves in the desert.

Jesus responds to the crowd with pity, seeing them as sheep in need of a shepherd. With Jesus, the shepherd, preaching late into the day, the disciples become anxious about the hour and the people's need for food. Jesus tells them to feed the crowd. Because their faith is still weak, they answer in worldly, almost sarcastic terms, asking Jesus if he expects them to have enough money to feed so many people. When Jesus asks how many loaves they have, they respond that they have five loaves and two fish, certainly not enough for such a large crowd.

The manner in which Jesus takes the loaves, raises his eyes to heaven, blesses the bread, breaks it, and gives it to his disciples to distribute foreshadows the celebration of the Eucharist. It also recalls the events of the Last Supper. That the disciples, not Jesus, distribute the food points to the disciples' special ministry in the celebration of the Eucharist. Jesus provides the gifts, but the disciples distribute them. The twelve baskets left recall the twelve tribes of Israel, thus linking this action with the promise to Israel in the Old Testament. The scene also recalls the feeding of the Israelites with manna in the desert during the time of the Exodus (16:4–16). Every meal story in the gospels has a message about the eucharistic celebration.

6:45–56 Jesus Walks on Water

As Jesus dismisses the crowd, a sense of urgency arises when he insists his disciples get into a boat and set out for Bethsaida, which is on the other side of the lake. Mark tells us Jesus then goes to an unnamed mountain to pray. Mark gives two signals that something significant is about to happen: Jesus goes up a mountain, a place where God meets with the prophets. Jesus also prays, as he often does before important events.

That evening Jesus saw the disciples struggling against a strong headwind. There is no mention of a storm as in other gospels. The disciples suddenly see Jesus walking on the water, and their first thought is that they're seeing a ghost. Terrified, they cry out, and Jesus bids them not to fear. When he speaks, he echoes the words of God, who appeared to Moses in a burning bush (Exodus 3:14). God said to Moses, "I am," and Jesus says to his disciples, "It is I." He gets into the boat, and the wind dies down.

The actions of Jesus walking on the water and calming the wind reveal his divine power. Mark, however, explicitly describes the closed minds of Jesus' disciples, who were astounded and still didn't understand the miracle of the multiplication of the loaves. Mark points to Jesus' divinity in two ways, namely the walking on water and the implication that Jesus is the eternal "I AM." He professes a faith the disciples will fully grasp only after Jesus' resurrection.

Mark ends this section with a summary of miracles and the crowd's overwhelming response. Jesus and his disciples arrive at Gennesaret. Crowds bring the sick to Jesus for healing. Either Jesus heals them, or they are healed by touching his garments. Wherever he goes, he encounters people who need healing. The crowd's strong faith stands in sharp contrast to the frail faith of Jesus' disciples. Mark continues to emphasize the need for faith in those who wish to be Jesus' disciples.

Review Questions

1. What message about faith do we get from the story about Jesus' return to his hometown?
2. What prompts Herod to kill John the Baptist?
3. How is John the Baptist's death a foreshadowing of Jesus' death?
4. What instructions do Jesus give the Twelve when he sent them on a mission?
5. What happens when the Twelve returned from their mission?
6. What is the eucharistic message behind the feeding of 5,000 in the desert?
7. How do Jesus' disciples react when he walks toward them on the water?

Closing Prayer (SEE PAGE 18)

Pray the closing prayer now or after *lectio divina*.

Lectio Divina (SEE PAGE 11)

Relax your body and maintain a posture of prayer (back straight, eyes shut, feet flat on the floor). This exercise can take as long as you want, but in the context of this Bible study, 10 to 20 minutes should be sufficient.

The meditations that follow are provided only to help group participants use this prayer form, but note that *lectio* is intended to bring one to a place of prayerful contemplation where the Word of God speaks to the hearer from his or her heart. (See page 11 for further instruction.)

Jesus' Rejection at Nazareth (6:1–6)

Faith allows God to act in our lives. Jesus teaches this in a positive manner as he heals people who have faith; he teaches it in a negative manner when he isn't able to perform miracles because of the people's lack of faith. When we pray, we pray with faith that God wants to answer our prayer in some manner. Faith enables us to believe God is answering our prayer even if we don't see that answer. Faith tells us God loves us and wants to help us. Faith, hope, and love are the foundation of our lives as Christians.

✠ *What can I learn from this passage?*

Mission of the Twelve (6:7–13)

Jesus sent the Twelve out as beggars, each with only one walking stick, one set of clothing, and one pair of sandals so nothing would distract them. This may seem harsh, but it offers a challenge. We live in a world of many luxuries. We should take an occasional look at our possessions and ask whether they distract us from or help us move closer to Christ. This could be a challenging examination for us.

✠ *What can I learn from this passage?*

Death of John the Baptist (6:14–29)

Just as Mark links John's life and death with Jesus' life and death, we link our lives with Jesus' life, death, and resurrection. Jesus began his mission when John was imprisoned, and now John's death foreshadows Jesus'. The rumor of John's resurrection will be overshadowed by the reality of Jesus' resurrection. Jesus picks up where John left off, and we pick up where Jesus left off—at his ascension. We journey with Jesus as our companion and the Spirit as our guide. Jesus' life continues with each of us.

✠ *What can I learn from this passage?*

Feeding 5,000 in the Desert (6:30–44)

We know how important the Eucharist is for Christianity. This passage tells us that when Jesus saw the large crowd, "his heart was moved with pity for them, for they were like sheep without a shepherd; and he began to teach them many things." Jesus offers us the Eucharist because he is the good shepherd who has pity for the sheep. We need help dedicating our lives to Christ and his message. Jesus gives us that help. Just as he fed 5,000 in the desert, he feeds us with heavenly food that gives us the strength to be faithful to him and his message.

✠ *What can I learn from this passage?*

Jesus Walks on Water (6:45–56)

This passage shows several images of Jesus as Lord. He goes up a mountain, which is where God visited Moses and other prophets. He prays, and that evening when the disciples are far out at sea, Jesus can still see them. Mark is alluding to Jesus' divine power. Jesus walks on water—the abode of evil spirits—an event that shows he has power over evil spirits. He's about to pass his disciples, but they must be the ones to cry out. In prayer, we call out to God for help. In response to his disciples, Jesus uses the phrase "It is I," another way by which he identifies his divinity. When he gets into the boat, the wind dies and all becomes peaceful. This Scripture passage challenges us to reflect on our image of Jesus' presence today.

✠ *What can I learn from this passage?*

PART 2: INDIVIDUAL STUDY (MARK 7—8:26)

Day 1: The Tradition of the Elders (7:1–23)

One major controversy in the early Church concerned the extent to which Gentiles observe Jewish prescriptions of the Law of Moses. Mark, writing for a mostly Gentile Christian audience, places Jesus at the center of this conflict. Judaism accepted the Pharisees as interpreters of the Law. Unfortunately, they added so many interpretations that people couldn't know all of them. In this passage, Jesus confronts this practice.

Mark describes the practices of the Jews as though his readers were not familiar with the customs and, indeed, many Gentile converts were not. Originally, only priests had to wash their hands before eating, but the Pharisees applied the obligation to all people. Mark says the Pharisees and some scribes from Jerusalem gathered around Jesus. The Jews from Jerusalem tended to follow the Law more rigidly than Jews who lived outside Palestine.

The Pharisees accuse Jesus' disciples of not washing their hands before eating. Jesus condemns the Pharisees by quoting Isaiah, who warned that people pay lip service while their heart is far removed from God (29:13) and teach human laws as though they were God's laws. Jesus points to a gift dedicated to God known as *qorban*. According to God's Law, a person must honor one's father and mother, but according to the human-made law of *qorban*, people who dedicate gifts to God no longer have to share them with their parents. In this way, the Pharisees actually supplanted God's command with a human command. Jesus declares that this is not the only time the Pharisees have supplanted God's Law.

Mark lists the sins that make a person impure. In the early Church, a strong debate took place between Jewish and Gentile converts to Christianity. Jewish Christians believed Jewish dietary laws should be followed, while Gentile Christians argued that these laws did not bind Christians. Mark, quoting Jesus, shows that Jewish dietary laws are no longer binding for Christianity. Jesus says it's not what enters the mouth that matters—it's what comes out of it. What goes into the mouth enters the stomach, but what comes out of the mouth comes from the heart.

Some commentators doubt Jesus spoke so explicitly about dietary laws because his words would have silenced the controversy in the early Church and made the change more acceptable to Jewish converts. But it was only after a long, difficult struggle that the Church decided to make exceptions to Jewish dietary laws, and Mark is most likely reporting the point as it was practiced and preached at the time he wrote his gospel.

Lectio Divina

Spend 8 to 10 minutes in silent contemplation of the following passage:

In Acts of the Apostles, Peter the apostle falls into a trance and has a vision of a large sheet coming down from heaven with four-legged animals, reptiles, and birds. A voice tells him to slaughter and eat what was on the sheet. Peter refuses, claiming he has never eaten anything unclean. The voice answers, "What God has made clean, you are not to call profane" (10:15). The purpose of the vision was not to get Peter to eat something that would harm him, but to tell him that God no longer wanted Jewish laws burdening Gentile converts. Gentiles ate certain foods, like pigs, that Jews refused to eat. God's love was inviting all good people to share in faith in Christ with as few obstacles as possible.

✠ *What can I learn from this passage?*

Day 2: The Canaanite Woman (7:24–30)

Jesus travels to the district of Tyre. Despite his desire to stay at a house in secret, a Greek woman—a Syrophoenician who is a Gentile—pays him homage, and begs for an exorcism for her daughter. Jesus, in a surprising and terse statement, tells her to feed the children first, since it's not right to take bread from children and throw it to the dogs. Here, the word *children* refers to the Israelites Jesus is preaching to. Totally out of character, Jesus hurls an insult at the woman, perhaps to test her. The Jews often used the word *dog* as a derogatory name for Gentiles. The woman ignores Jesus' response, replying that even dogs eat what falls from the table. Her faith is so strong that she dares to debate Jesus in true rabbinical fashion. She knows that even a few crumbs from Jesus will be powerful enough to heal her daughter. Jesus, pleased by her faith and her response, sends her home, telling her the demon has left her daughter. The woman could have believed Jesus said this just to get rid of her, but she trusts Jesus' words and goes home to find the demon cast out of her daughter.

Lectio Divina

Spend 8 to 10 minutes in silent contemplation of the following passage:

> After Jesus' resurrection, the Church was much more successful in spreading Jesus' message among the Gentiles than among the Jews. The story of the Gentile woman shows Jesus' concern for a Gentile who demonstrates strong faith. The story also teaches another lesson: Jesus needn't be present to perform a healing. He doesn't go near the woman's daughter, but he heals from afar. For us, it's a message that we pray with confidence even when we never see or hear Jesus Christ.

> ✠ *What can I learn from this passage?*

Day 3: The Healing of the "Deaf Mute" (7:31–37)

Jesus travels on a perplexing roundabout journey through Gentile territory, going east, north, and finally southeast. Mark may want to show that Jesus' mission was not just to the Jews, but to all people—many people in the territory of Galilee weren't Jews. Some commentators believe the circuitous route indicates that Jesus was willing to go out of his way to reach as many people as he could. Others feel Mark wasn't as familiar with Palestine as other gospel writers were.

People bring a man with hearing and speech impairments to Jesus and beg him to lay hands on the man. Just as the paralyzed man had others bring him to Jesus, the deaf man has others bring him to Jesus. Jesus leads the man away from the crowd and performs this miracle in private.

He uses the actions of Jewish healers of the day, putting "his fingers into the man's ears and, spitting, touched his tongue." Jesus looks toward heaven, the throne of God, and lets out a sigh that expresses the deaf man's pain. With the same authority he would use to cast out demons, Jesus commands the man's ears to open. The man is then able to hear and speak clearly. Even though Jesus tells the man not to let others know what Jesus did, the man spreads the word about the miracle.

While the method of healing Jesus used was common at that time, it has additional significance. When Jesus puts his spittle on the deaf man's tongue, something inside Jesus is transferred to the inside of the other person. The deaf man shares in the life of Jesus, which makes him able to hear with the ears of faith.

Mark is saying that, just as this Gentile was able to hear and speak, after Jesus' resurrection many Gentiles would hear Jesus' message and speak about it to others. The image of deafness and blindness in the New Testament has a spiritual undertone, pointing to hearing with understanding and seeing with faith. In 4:9, Jesus declares, "Whoever has ears to hear." The man not only hears with his ears; he understands the spiritual message he hears.

Lectio Divina

Spend 8 to 10 minutes in silent contemplation of the following passage:

Paul, writing to the Romans, says, "How can they hear without someone to preach?" (4:10). Jesus opens the ears of the deaf man to hear his message—not just to hear his words, but to hear with the ears of faith. Preaching is not done just from the pulpit, but from the actions and words of Christians. This message underlines the importance of living, worshiping, and believing in a way that shows others how Christianity influences us. As Jesus told us, we must let our light shine before others that they may hear and see God's Word.

✠ *What can I learn from this passage?*

Day 4: Jesus Feeds 4,000 (8:1–10)

After preaching to a large crowd in an area far from their homes, Jesus expresses his compassionate concern for the people because they've been with him for three days with nothing to eat. The number three often means something has taken place. In this case, it would mean that the people are definitely hungry. In both stories about feeding a large crowd, we read that Jesus heart was moved with pity for the people. In a previous story, Jesus fed 5,000 people in Jewish territory, and he now feeds 4,000 people in the desert in Gentile territory. Although the disciples should have known Jesus fed the 5,000, Mark shows they still lack understanding when they ask how they can feed so many in this deserted area.

The significant number in the Jewish-territory multiplication of the loaves is twelve, because the twelve baskets remaining refer to the twelve tribes of Israel. The significant number for the Gentiles is seven, the number of perfection. In the desert in Gentile territory, when Jesus asks how many loaves the disciples have, they declare that they have seven loaves. After all the people have eaten, the disciples fill seven baskets with leftover fragments. The number seven points to the Eucharist as the perfect gift, and the seven baskets left underline the abundance of blessings coming from the eucharistic meal.

Jesus performs the miracle in the same manner as in the story of the multiplication of the loaves. He takes the loaves, gives thanks, breaks them, and gives them to the disciples to distribute. An abundance is left. Jesus dismisses the crowd as in the other story and moves on to another region.

It's no accident that the story of feeding 4,000 Gentiles sounds much like the feeding of 5,000 in the Jewish context. Mark uses parallel stories called *doublets*. In the first series of stories, we have (a) the multiplication of loaves for 5,000; (b) the crossing of the water; (c) the confrontation with the Pharisees; (d) the food intended first for the Jews; and (e) the healing of the hearing- and speech-impaired man. In this second series of stories, we have (a) the multiplication of loaves for 4,000; (b) the crossing of the water; (c) the confrontation with the Pharisees; (d) the leaven of the Pharisees; and (e) the healing of the blind man. Mark has taken these stories from the early Church and purposely structured them in doublets.

Lectio Divina

Spend 8 to 10 minutes in silent contemplation of the following passage:

The multiplication of loaves for the Jews and Gentiles reminds us that the Eucharist is for all people. Jesus sat at the table with sinners and saints, and he now shares the Eucharist with Jews and Gentiles. The celebration of the Eucharist is meant to embrace everyone. As in the previous story, Jesus' disciples—not Jesus—distribute the bread, signifying that the Church, the Body of Christ, is the proper distributor of the Eucharist. The story is about people who ate and were satisfied. Jesus offers the Eucharist to satisfy our spiritual longing for union with him.

✠ *What can I learn from this passage?*

Day 5: The Leaven of the Pharisees (8:11–21)

Jesus crosses the water with his disciples and returns to Jewish territory. The Pharisees and the people expected some sign to accompany the coming of the Messiah, and they ask Jesus for such a sign. Mark stresses Jesus' humanness when he says Jesus lets out a deep sigh and answers that no sign will be coming. In his frustration, Jesus emphasizes his refusal by prefacing it with "Amen, I say to you." Jesus has already performed many signs that show him to be the fulfillment of the Old Testament promise, but the Pharisees have closed their minds to these signs. A frustrated Jesus and his disciples go off to another shore.

Mark continues to illustrate the depth of the disciples' lack of understanding of Jesus and Jesus' growing frustration. They have one loaf with them in the boat, and when Jesus warns them against the leaven of the Pharisees and Herod, the disciples mistakenly believe Jesus is referring to their lack of bread. Actually, Jesus is warning against the influence of the Pharisees and Herod and their hypocritical ways. Jesus' irritation shows when he asks whether they are blind or deaf and whether they remember the multiplication of the loaves. Mark could be posing these questions here for his readers, who must answer each question for themselves. How strong is *their* understanding after hearing about Jesus? Jesus' continued frustration with his disciples underlines his human side.

Lectio Divina

Spend 8 to 10 minutes in silent contemplation of the following passage:

When Jesus warns his disciples against the leaven of the Pharisees, he is actually warning them not to follow the Pharisees' example. The Pharisees give an external example of holiness by following the precepts of the Law, but their hearts are far from loving God. The Pharisees we meet in the gospels seek to *look* good rather than *be* good. They are self-righteous, judging others' conduct and believing themselves to be better than others. This is the leaven of the Pharisees. Jesus is warning us not to become self-righteous or judgmental. Holiness consists of recognizing that we are made to the image and likeness of God, not the image and likeness of the self-righteous or judgmental.

✠ *What can I learn from this passage?*

Day 6: A Blind Man at Bethsaida (8:22–26)

When Jesus arrives in Bethsaida, some people bring a blind man to him so Jesus can touch and heal him. The blind man, like the deaf man Jesus healed in an earlier part of the gospel (7:31–37), is also brought to Jesus by others. The story of the blind man is not only a doublet with the story of the healing of the deaf person with the speech impediment (7:31–37), but it also serves as a transition story in the Gospel of Mark. Jesus uses the same healing method here as he does with the deaf man with the speech impairment. He takes the blind man off privately and puts spittle on his eyes. The man first sees people who look like walking trees, and when Jesus touches his eyes for a second time, the man sees clearly.

The blind man is a symbol of the disciples' growth in understanding. They've been blind about Jesus' identity up to this point. Now they'll begin to understand, but still not clearly. Like the first step in the healing of the blind man, the disciples' understanding of Jesus is a blurry picture. For the disciples, from now on each step is a gradual unfolding of Jesus' true mission. Jesus sends the formerly blind man home and orders him to keep away from the village so he won't spread the news of the miracle.

Lectio Divina

Spend 8 to 10 minutes in silent contemplation of the following passage:

Reflection on the Scriptures is important for us to grow in faith, hope, and love, but the picture is never fully complete until our life ends. We journey with Jesus to deepen our understanding of Jesus' life and message. Reading and studying Scripture helps us understand more each day. Keeping our mind on Jesus while not becoming blind to God's presence in our day-to-day lives, especially during difficult moments, helps us see more clearly. Jesus is with us every moment, even now as we are reading and studying. It's impossible to think of Jesus every moment, but we can draw our minds frequently to his presence in creation. As long as we periodically recognize Jesus' presence, each day is a day of prayer.

✠ *What can I learn from this passage?*

Review Questions

1. Where did the law demanding that Jews wash their hands before eating originate?
2. What is the central issue of Jesus' controversy with the Pharisees and scribes concerning the tradition of the elders?
3. Why is Jesus concerned about the law of eating certain foods and abstaining from others?
4. What messages are found in the story of the Syrophoenician woman?
5. What is significant about the manner in which Jesus heals the deaf man?
6. Why does Jesus get upset when the Pharisees asks for a sign?
7. What does Jesus mean when he speaks of the leaven of the Pharisees?
8. What is the significance of the healing of the blind man of Bethsaida in Mark's Gospel?

Revealing the Mystery

MARK 8:27—9:32

This kind can only come out through prayer. (9:29)

Opening Prayer (SEE PAGE 18)

Context

Part 1: Mark 8:27—9:8 Peter professes that Jesus is the Christ, but when Jesus predicts his passion, death, and resurrection, Peter rebukes him. Jesus insults Peter, calling him a Satan for thinking in human rather than godly terms. He admonishes his disciples to pick up their cross and follow him. They shouldn't seek to profit the whole world and lose their soul. They shouldn't be ashamed of professing faith in Jesus, thus making Christ ashamed of them. Jesus takes Peter, James, and John up a mountain and is transfigured before their eyes. He is glorified, with Moses and Elijah on either side. The vision ends as suddenly as it began.

Part 2: Mark 9:9–32 Jesus and his disciples come down the mountain as Jesus says Elijah has come. The allusion seems to be to John the Baptist. When they arrive at the bottom of the mountain, they encounter a possessed boy. Jesus must cast out the demon because the disciples are powerless. Jesus says this kind of demon can be cast out only through prayer. For a second time, Jesus predicts his passion, death, and resurrection.

PART 1: GROUP STUDY (MARK 8:27—9:8)

Read aloud Mark 8:27—9:8.

8:27–30 Peter's Confession About Jesus

Jesus and his disciples travel toward Caesarea Philippi, which is situated at the foot of Mount Hermon, an extreme northern point of Palestine. Mark places Peter's profession of faith at the center of his gospel, where a change in the disciples' understanding of Jesus is still evolving. When Jesus asks his disciples "Who do people say that I am?," they reply with some of the names given in an earlier chapter (see Mark 6:14–16). Some say John the Baptist; others say Elijah, a prophet the Jewish people expected to return before the coming of the Messiah; or a prophet like Moses, who is spoken of in the Book of Deuteronomy (18:15–18). Peter correctly identifies Jesus as the Messiah but makes no mention of Jesus' divinity as found in Matthew's Gospel (16:16). The disciples hadn't yet reached an understanding of Jesus as the Son of God. As usual, Jesus orders his disciples to keep silent about his identity.

8:31–33 The First Prediction of the Passion

After Peter identifies Jesus as the Messiah, Jesus makes his first prediction of his passion, death, and resurrection. Note Jesus never speaks of his passion and death without also mentioning his resurrection, which makes the total picture of salvation the Good News. In Mark's Gospel, Jesus predicts his death and resurrection three times (8:31, 9:31, 10:33–34), shedding light on Jesus' true mission of the Messiah. Peter, however, rejects such an idea and rebukes Jesus for predicting such a tragedy. Peter is unwittingly trying to lure Jesus from the true fulfillment of his ministry in the same manner as Satan in the temptation story. This is why Jesus addresses Peter as "Satan" when he harshly rebukes Peter for his lack of understanding. This event also recalls the story of the blind man: Like the other disciples, Peter is arriving at his understanding of Jesus and his mission only gradually.

8:34—9:1 The Meaning of Discipleship

Mark will follow the three predictions of Jesus' death and resurrection with three discourses by Jesus on discipleship (8:34—9:1, 9:35–50, 10:42–45). In this first of the three discourses, Jesus speaks to the crowds as well as to his disciples. By including the crowds, Mark reminds his readers that Jesus is not only speaking to the disciples of his day, but also to future disciples.

Mark links several sayings spoken by Jesus at different times. The true disciple must deny oneself, take up the cross, and follow Jesus. Although Jesus suffered, died, and was raised, Mark warns the members of the early Christian community that they shouldn't believe that all evil has been conquered or that all suffering has ended. Just as Jesus suffered, they must be willing to suffer and carry their cross.

That reference to carrying one's cross is most likely a postresurrection saying—Jesus' disciples would not have identified a cross with Jesus until he was crucified.

Jesus warns that those striving to save their earthly lives could lose eternal life in the process, while those willing to suffer the loss of their earthly life for the sake of Jesus will gain eternal life. The message in Mark is directed to the persecuted as well as to all Jesus' disciples who read his words. If a person is "ashamed" to proclaim his or her faith in Christ in the midst of persecution, Jesus will treat that person the same way at judgment time. When Jesus uses the term "Son of Man" in this passage, he speaks of himself in his messianic image as the one who suffers, dies, and is raised, and as the one who will call his followers to eternal life at the end of time. The image of the Son of Man links Jesus with the suffering servant in the Book of Isaiah.

Many people in the early Church believed that the end of the world would come soon. Mark apparently expresses this belief when he states that some of those who hear these words will still be alive at the Second Coming of Christ. Although Jesus says at the beginning of the gospel that the kingdom of God has come, here he speaks of when "the kingdom of God has come in power."

9:2–8 The Transfiguration of Jesus

Many commentators believe the transfiguration is a postresurrection story Mark placed within Jesus' ministry to inform readers that the Jesus who was raised was the same Jesus who had lived among the disciples. Other commentators believe the transfiguration was meant to present a preview of Jesus' resurrection and a sign of Jesus' divinity. That Jesus would choose Peter, James, and John to accompany him up the mountain underlines the significance of this event.

The transfiguration takes place on a high mountain, a place of visitation from God throughout the Old Testament (see Exodus 3:1–6). Jesus acquires a heavenly countenance as he is transfigured. Mark adds a human touch by telling us that Jesus' garments are whiter than anyone on Earth could bleach them—they had a whiteness only heaven could bring about, a whiteness of glory. Elijah, who represented the prophets of the Old Testament, and Moses, who represented the Law, are seen conversing with Jesus.

Peter proposes that they build three dwellings on the mountain for Jesus, Moses, and Elijah, perhaps as part of the Greek custom of building a shrine where a deity appeared. Mark mentions that Peter is terrified, a common reaction to a visitation from God. Clouds often accompanied visitations of a deity. In the Old Testament, the Ark of the Covenant, which contained elements sacred to the people of Israel and which was understood to be the Lord's footstool, rested in the midst of the Israelite community in a tent. When a cloud descended on the tent, people knew the glory of God was filling the tent (see Exodus 40:34–38).

Although Peter recognizes that something great is happening in their midst, he never suspects Jesus' true identity. A cloud overshadows them just as it overshadowed the tent containing the Ark of the Covenant, and from the cloud comes a voice proclaiming that Jesus is God's beloved Son, to whom they should listen. The words heard only by Jesus at his baptism (1:11) are now heard by the three disciples. The vision ends with dramatic simplicity: The three suddenly find themselves alone with Jesus.

Review Questions

1. Who does Peter say Jesus is?
2. What happens when Peter rebukes Jesus for predicting his passion, death, and resurrection?
3. What is a major condition for discipleship?
4. What happens at Jesus' transfiguration?

Closing Prayer (SEE PAGE 18)

Pray the closing prayer now or after *lectio divina*.

Lectio Divina (SEE PAGE 11)

Relax your body and maintain a posture of prayer (back straight, eyes shut, feet flat on the floor). This exercise can take as long as you want, but in the context of this Bible study, 10 to 20 minutes should be sufficient.

The meditations that follow are provided only to help group participants use this prayer form, but note that *lectio* is intended to bring one to a place of prayerful contemplation where the Word of God speaks to the hearer from his or her heart. (See page 11 for further instruction.)

Peter's Confession About Jesus (8:27–30)

Jesus' disciples have now been traveling with him for a while, but they still struggle to understand Jesus' identity. A big step comes when Peter proclaims Jesus as the Messiah, but he must still learn the meaning of the term. We become Christians through baptism, but we face the same challenge Peter faced: What does it mean to be Christian? The real challenge of being Christian isn't just knowing the name or knowing about Jesus—it means living Jesus' message. Peter could say Jesus was the Messiah, but he had no idea what that meant. Jesus gradually teaches the disciples what the term *Messiah* ("Christ") means. In the same way, Christians learn the full meaning of being disciples as we struggle, suffer, worship, celebrate, and reach out to others as Christ did. It's one thing to be known as Christian, but it's another to live as a Christian.

✠ *What can I learn from this passage?*

The First Prediction of the Passion (8:31–33)

In his first prediction of his passion, death, and resurrection, Jesus gives a full picture of what it means to be the Messiah. Peter doesn't like what he hears and dares to rebuke Jesus, but Jesus turns on Peter and rebukes him harshly. Like Jesus, we must be willing to offer ourselves for the sake of others, even if it means dying for our faith. Most of us won't have to face death for our faith, but we have the obligation to love God and neighbor as ourselves, willingly spending ourselves for the sake of those in need. We bear the title "Christian," so we should act like Christ in all we do.

✠ *What can I learn from this passage?*

The Meaning of Discipleship (8:34—9:1)

We must be willing to carry our cross as Jesus carried his. Carrying a cross doesn't necessarily demand suffering, but it does demand dedication. We all have responsibilities, and faithfully living up to them while helping others is a form of carrying our cross. We experience irritations, inconveniences, frustrations, anger, grief, false accusations, and other challenges we must endure with patience and love. This can indeed be a cross. Like Jesus, we must be willing to endure all suffering as Christians. Jesus didn't solve all the problems of the world. We must never be ashamed of being known as Christian. We must pick up our crosses, do our share, and accept the suffering and pain of life in union with Christ. Many joyful moments will help us endure our crosses.

✠ *What can I learn from this passage?*

The Transfiguration of Jesus (9:2–8)

Because Christians believe Jesus is the Christ, the Son of God, we view the world differently than those who don't believe. In a sense, we transfigure creation. We see the hand of God in the noise of the city, the warmth of the country, the blue of the sky, and in every aspect of creation. We live by what we see with our physical eyes and with the eyes of faith. A tragic event leads us to pray for the safety of the victims, and a joyful event leads us to thank God for that joy. We know and believe Jesus is with us even though we see him only through the eyes of faith.

✠ *What can I learn from this passage?*

PART 2: INDIVIDUAL STUDY (MARK 9:9–32)

Day 1: The Coming of Elijah (9:9–13)

The members of the early Church community must have wondered why no one seemed to know about the transfiguration during Jesus' lifetime. Mark answers their question by showing that Jesus ordered his disciples not to tell anyone about the vision until he rose from the dead. This is in keeping with the messianic secret dominant in the Gospel of Mark. Mark links Jesus' transfiguration with his death and resurrection, just as the glory of Jesus' resurrection will only be truly understood in light of Jesus' passion and death.

The three disciples wonder what "rising from the dead" means. They question Jesus about Elijah, noting that the learned scribes of the day expected Elijah to return before the "day of the LORD" (Malachi 3:23). In the Old Testament, we don't read about Elijah's dying—we read that he "went up to heaven in a whirlwind" (2 Kings 2:11). When the members of the early Church realized Jesus was the Messiah, they had the same question about Elijah, as did the disciples: *Did Elijah return?* Mark has the disciples ask this question for the members of the early Church as well as for themselves. Jesus alludes to John the Baptist as Elijah without naming John. John came not only to prepare the way of the Lord by his words, but also by the events of his life. Just as John had to suffer and die, Jesus will too. Mark is revealing that Jesus' true disciples are willing to suffer and die as Jesus did to share in the glory of resurrection.

Lectio Divina

Spend 8 to 10 minutes in silent contemplation of the following passage:

In our postresurrection faith, we expect to share in the resurrection with Christ. We have the privilege of understanding Christ's message but, as usual, with every spiritual privilege comes a spiritual obligation. Our attitude toward life and death is expanded when we believe we will rise in Christ after we die. Once we believe this, we develop a concern for others, praying not only for our own glorious resurrection, but for the glorious resurrection of others. As Christians, we pray for the dead and the dying, believing our prayers help those we pray for. We may ponder how our belief in resurrection affects our actions here and now.

✠ *What can I learn from this passage?*

Day 2: The Healing of a Possessed Boy (9:14–29)

When Jesus comes down the mountain after the transfiguration, he confronts the same problem Moses confronted when he came down the mountain after God visited him (see Exodus 32). Moses found that the people had lost faith and turned to a false image. Jesus finds that his disciples, who had already cast out demons, don't have enough faith to cast the demon out of a possessed boy. They had apparently tried, but now the scribes argue with them about their failure. The boy's father came to seek Jesus' help, but in Jesus' absence sought help from his disciples. Mark doesn't hesitate to show the human side of Jesus, who in frustration addresses questions about how much longer he must endure such a faithless generation.

Mark's description of the possessed boy gives the impression of someone having an epileptic seizure. The boy foams at the mouth, grinds his teeth, and becomes rigid as the demon casts him to the ground. The father's faith is evidently weak: He addresses Jesus as "teacher" rather than "lord," and asks for a cure "if you can do anything." When Jesus rebukes the father for his lack of faith, the father accepts the rebuke and responds, "I do believe, help my unbelief!" When the evil spirit recognizes Jesus, it throws the boy into another convulsion so Jesus has to command the spirit to leave the boy.

The gathering crowd seems to force Jesus to perform the exorcism quickly, perhaps to keep secret his messianic mission. Because the boy had only periodic seizures, Jesus orders the evil spirit out of the boy and commands it never to return. The boy appears dead, but Jesus raises him to a new life free of the power of the evil spirit. This is the fourth and final exorcism recorded in Mark's Gospel.

When the disciples later ask Jesus why they were unable to perform this exorcism, Jesus says they can cast out demons only by the power of prayer. When Mark speaks of prayer, he presumes that faith is always present when one prays. Jesus' words remind readers that casting out evil spirits is an act of God and not an action Jesus' disciples can perform through their own power.

Lectio Divina

Spend 8 to 10 minutes in silent contemplation of the following passage:

> The father of the man with epilepsy realizes his faith is weak. He declares "I do believe," but he admits the weakness of his faith when he adds "help my unbelief." The struggle of believing with a strong faith is a challenge for all of us. That father's prayer has become the prayer of many people: "Lord, I do believe, help my unbelief." Jesus' disciples believed God had given them the power to cast out demons when they were on their missionary journey, but their need for greater faith at this time matched that of the boy's father. We do believe, but when our faith wanes, we must call out for greater faith.

✠ *What can I learn from this passage?*

Day 3: The Second Prediction of the Passion (9:30–32)

Up to this point, Jesus has kept his messianic secret but has allowed the crowds to follow him. In this section, Jesus travels secretly through Galilee toward Jerusalem and the passion. On the journey he continues to teach his disciples about his betrayal, death, and resurrection, again using the term "Son of Man" to identify himself with Isaiah's suffering servant. Jesus notes that he will be "handed over," most likely a reference to Judas' betrayal. He notes that men will kill him but that he will be raised three days after his death.

Jesus never speaks of his passion and death without adding the message about his resurrection. This is an important message from Mark as he presents the Good News of Jesus Christ, the Son of God, to the persecuted: Many of them will suffer and die, but it's not the end—they'll be raised with Christ.

The shadow of the cross is more evident in Mark's Gospel. Despite repeated lessons from Jesus, the disciples still don't understand him, but they're afraid to ask for an explanation. Although the disciples make this journey with Jesus, Jesus must journey with the reality that he is emotion-ally alone, with no one to understand his frightening destiny.

Lectio Divina

Spend 8 to 10 minutes in silent contemplation of the following passage:

The cross has a different meaning now than it had during Jesus' life. We have the advantage of knowing that the cross doesn't symbolize something totally evil. It's a challenge by which we prove our love for God and for one another. Jesus brought glory to the cross and meaning to suffering and death. We must pick up our crosses and follow Jesus.

✠ *What can I learn from this passage?*

Review Questions

1. Why do the people expect Elijah to come before Jesus?
2. What happens when Jesus comes down the mountain after his transfiguration?
3. What does Jesus say in his second prediction of his passion?

The Mystery Fully Revealed

MARK 9:33–10

Taking a child he placed it in their midst, and putting his arms around it he said to them, "Whoever receives one child such as this in my name, receives me; and whoever receives me, receives not me but the One who sent me." (9:36–37)

Opening Prayer (SEE PAGE 18)

Context

Part 1: Mark 9:33—10:12 The disciples are embarrassed when Jesus catches them arguing about who is the greatest. Jesus tells them the first shall be the servant of all. As an example, he urges them to receive a child as though they are receiving Christ. When they ask what they should do about someone who is driving out demons in Jesus' name but who isn't one with them, Jesus tells them that those who aren't against them are for them. To lead a newcomer to the faith into sin is so terrible that it would be better for that person to drown with a millstone around his neck. People should sacrifice a limb rather than sin with it. Jesus speaks of the sacredness of marriage when he declares that from the beginning, God made human beings male and female and that the two become one.

Part 2: Mark 10:13–52 Jesus says the reign of God belongs to those who are like children. When a rich man who has kept all the commandments comes to Jesus, Jesus invites him to abandon his wealth and become one of Jesus' followers. When the rich man can't bring himself to do it, Jesus says it's hard for a rich person to enter the reign of God. But with God, all things are possible. For the third time, Jesus predicts his passion, death, and resurrection. Disciples James and John ignore all Jesus has taught and ask if they can sit at his right and left in his kingdom. Jesus teaches them and all the disciples that just as he came to serve and give his life, they should too.

PART 1: GROUP STUDY (MARK 9:33—10:12)

Read aloud Mark 9:33—10:12.

9:33–37 The Least Among You

Mark links many of Jesus' messages. Each message confronts a weakness found in discipleship. At Capernaum, where Jesus began his ministry, he becomes aware that his disciples are arguing about who is the greatest. When he asks about the argument they remain silent, recognizing that their answer will reveal that they are motivated by ambition rather than by humbly following Jesus. Mark, aware Jesus' message is for all his disciples—including Mark's readers—introduces another lesson about the true meaning of discipleship. To be first in the kingdom of God, they must accept the position of being the least of all and the servants of all. His kingdom isn't like worldly kingdoms—it's a kingdom of service.

Jesus places a child in the midst of the disciples, embraces the child, and says they must accept even those as socially insignificant as this child, who has no special rank. In receiving a child in Jesus' name they receive Jesus, who comes without a special rank. In receiving Jesus, they receive the one who sent him.

9:38–41 Another Exorcist

The early Church community encountered non-Christian exorcists who used Jesus' name to cast out evil spirits. A rare occasion in the Gospel of Mark has John speaking alone to Jesus. John asks whether they should stop those who don't belong to their company from expelling demons in

Jesus' name. Jesus says that anyone able to perform exorcisms in his name, even though not explicitly professing faith in Jesus, must have some faith. Because this person isn't acting against Jesus, then the person must be for Jesus.

In the early Church, some of the people who preached in Christ's name hadn't yet celebrated the sacrament of baptism. They didn't preach against Christ, but spoke his message in a favorable manner. Mark speaks for these people and conveys Jesus' message that they shouldn't be stopped from performing their ministry.

As though John needs further comfort, Mark places another of Jesus' teachings at the end of the passage: Anyone who treats a follower of Christ with kindness *because* that person is a follower of Christ will be rewarded by God. In the previous passage, Jesus said that anyone who receives a child in his name receives him. In both cases, the reward comes with receiving someone in Christ's name.

9:42–50 Avoiding Temptation

New members of the faith are considered buds with a delicate faith. They are the "little ones," the simple believers who must be given good example. Jesus says it would be better to face a horrible death by drowning than to cause scandal to a budding follower of Jesus. Besides crucifixion, drowning was one of the most feared types of execution in Jesus' day. Jesus doesn't speak about an ordinary household millstone tied around the condemned person's neck, but a heavy millstone used by a beast of burden.

Causing another to lose faith is a sin so terrible that a person should take drastic steps to avoid doing it. Jesus speaks of cutting off a hand or a foot or plucking out an eye as better than suffering eternal damnation. When Jesus speaks of such radical maiming, he shouldn't be taken literally. The loss of one limb still leaves a person with another that can be the instrument of the sin. Jesus uses such strong imagery to illustrate the seriousness of sin. Christians must learn to control God's gifts of life and limb so they don't become an occasion of sin for others.

When Mark speaks of the fires and worms of Gehenna into which such a person will be plunged due to sin, he finds a ready quote in Isaiah 66:24 that speaks of the punishment of unquenchable fire and the worms that never die. The fire becomes the link to the next saying, a somewhat confusing statement about everyone's being salted by fire. Apparently this refers to the practice of salting a sacrifice before offering it to be burned. In the same manner, the true disciple should be a well-prepared sacrifice for God.

Mark uses the image of salt to continue his choice of Jesus' sayings in this section. The salt a disciple must keep in his or her heart is to live according to Jesus' message, which leaves one at peace with others. The true disciple avoids worldly ambition, haughtiness, or scandal and serves with the confidence, humility, and trust of a little child. Such a disciple will be "salted with fire," while one who seeks worldly ambitions will be like tasteless salt—a useless and weak disciple.

10:1–12 Marriage and Divorce

Jesus travels south toward Jerusalem into the area of Judea. Jesus had been traveling in secret, but now crowds gather and he teaches them openly. The Pharisees, who believe in divorce, ask whether it's right for a husband to divorce his wife. Mark mentions that they challenge Jesus as a test, showing that divorce was a sensitive topic. In the rabbinical fashion used in debates, Jesus answers their question with a question. He asks what Moses commanded, and they answer that Moses allowed divorce as long as a written notice of dismissal was given to the divorced woman. Moses' Law concerned a divorced woman who was married a second time but wished to return to her first husband. Moses forbade this, since the woman was considered "defiled" (Deuteronomy 24:1–4). Jesus tells his listeners that Moses allowed divorce not because it was God's will, but because of the people's stubbornness and inability to learn.

Jesus goes back to the very beginning of creation, when God's will was expressed most clearly. From the beginning, God made people male and female and declared that "the two of them become one body" (Genesis 2:24). Since no human being is greater than God, who established the idea of marriage, no one has a right to separate what God has joined.

Back at the house, Jesus further explains the message to the disciples. Adultery is a sin against the offended spouse. Until Mark wrote these words, few in Jesus' era would have spoken of an unfaithful husband as committing adultery against his wife. The Jews of Jesus' day believed that a married woman who had sexual relations with another man was committing adultery against her husband but that a man who had sexual relations with a married woman was committing adultery against the man she was married to.

Yet Jesus states that a man who divorces his wife and marries another commits adultery against her, and a woman who divorces her husband and marries another commits adultery against him. Women had more divorce rights in the Greek world, for which Mark wrote his gospel, than they did within Judaism. Mark most likely changed Jesus' words and spoke of women as having the right to divorce to convey a message to his Gentile audience.

Review Questions

1. What is Jesus' reaction when his disciples argue over who is the greatest?
2. How does Jesus respond when John asks whether they should stop someone who casts out devils in Jesus' name?
3. What does Jesus mean when he talks about cutting off a hand or foot or plucking out an eye?
4. Why does Jesus use the image of salt?
5. What does Jesus say about marriage and divorce?

Closing Prayer (SEE PAGE 18)

Pray the closing prayer now or after *lectio divina*.

Lectio Divina (SEE PAGE 11)

Relax your body and maintain a posture of prayer (back straight, eyes shut, feet flat on the floor). This exercise can take as long as you want, but in the context of this Bible study, 10 to 20 minutes should be sufficient.

The meditations that follow are provided only to help group participants use this prayer form, but note that *lectio* is intended to bring one to a place of prayerful contemplation where the Word of God speaks to the hearer from his or her heart. (See page 11 for further instruction.)

The Least Among You (9:33–37)

The call to discipleship is a call to service, not a call to power. Following Jesus' example, disciples are called to serve those who are weak, outcast, poor, or lonely. Discipleship demands helping those who have no means of repaying. On the other hand, the true disciple shouldn't ignore those in power or those who can repay, but the rewards of such service should not be the motive for serving. Disciples may seek positions of authority in government or even in the Church, but they should seek these positions for service and not for glory or power. Discipleship is service in the name of Christ.

✠ *What can I learn from this passage?*

Another Exorcist (9:38–41)

Jesus teaches that we share in ministry by something as simple as sharing a cup of cold water with those who belong to Christ, that is, disciples of Jesus Christ. Paul the apostle often exhorted believers to care for the needs of other believers, promising them a reward for such generous support of those in ministry. Those who minister do so willingly, but they are human and need our support and encouragement. In doing this, we share in their ministry.

✠ *What can I learn from this passage?*

Avoiding Temptation (9:42–50)

The image of salt recalls Jesus' words that we as Jesus' disciples are the salt of the Earth. Instead of leading others into sin, we are called to lead others to God. Instead of having to cut off a limb or pluck out an eye, we should use the gifts of touch, walking, and seeing to perform good actions. We are called to bring peace to the world, not sin. When we live in union with Christ, we are the salt of the Earth. Jesus tells us, "Keep salt in yourselves and you will have peace with one another." Sin leads to turmoil; living in union with Christ brings peace.

✠ *What can I learn from this passage?*

Marriage and Divorce (10:1–12)

The issue of divorce goes far back in history. God created man and woman to form a family. God made family the centerpiece of creation to the point that when a man and woman marry, they become one—and in becoming one, a family is born. A child is born into a family and becomes a member of a family. When we speak of divorce, we speak of the disruption of a family even if that family consists only of a husband and wife. Accordingly, Jesus can deny the Law of Moses and go back to the beginning and say, "Therefore what God has joined together, no human being must separate." The ideal of marriage becomes a blessing for some and a source of pain for those whose marriage dissolves. Jesus' words are not meant as a condemnation of those who are divorced, but as a support for God's plan for creation.

✠ *What can I learn from this passage?*

PART 2: INDIVIDUAL STUDY (MARK 10:13–52)

Day 1: Jesus Blesses Little Children (10:13–16)

Parents brought their children to Jesus so he would touch them for good health. Many view children as receiving what families give them but providing nothing in return. The disciples reflect the thinking of the day in rebuking the children, apparently trying to keep them from Jesus, but Jesus' reaction is surprisingly strong: He indignantly rebukes the disciples for trying to keep the children from him. He instructs his disciples about the need to be like little children, telling them that the kingdom of heaven belongs to such as these. He doesn't say that the kingdom belongs *only* to children, but to "such as these"—those who act with trust, humility, and love as children do. The true disciple must accept the kingdom of heaven with the virtues of a little child. Those who don't will not enter it. Jesus' human side again emerges as he embraces the children, blesses them, and lays hands on them.

Lectio Divina

Spend 8 to 10 minutes in silent contemplation of the following passage:

> Jesus calls us to become like children—not in the sense of being childish, but in the sense of practicing the natural childlike virtues of trust and love. Jesus is apparently caught up in the joy and playfulness of the children and shows a rare reaction of annoyance when the disciples rebuke the children. The scene is encouraging when we realize that Jesus is a visible image of the invisible God. This is God delighting in children. Children can cause the rest of us to smile easily, and they have the same effect on Jesus to the point that he says, "Let the children come to me; do not prevent them, for the kingdom of God belongs to such as these." Jesus calls us to trust and love as children do and to have a playful and cheerful response to the presence of God.

✠ *What can I learn from this passage?*

Day 2: The Dangers of Riches (10:17–31)

As Jesus sets out on a journey, a man runs to him and kneels before him in submission. Mark doesn't initially speak of the man as a rich man. The man addresses Jesus as "good teacher" and asks what he must do to gain eternal life. The Jews saw no one as being good except God. Since the man addresses Jesus as "teacher" and not "lord," he doesn't view Jesus as being more than a rabbi. Jesus challenges the title "good" and reminds the man of the reverence due to God alone.

When Jesus directs the man to follow the commandments of the covenant God made with Moses and the Jewish people, the man replies that he has done all these things since he was a child. Jesus looks on him with love and says the man lacks only one thing: He must give his possessions to the poor. Jesus then invites him to follow him. The man went away sad, because he had many possessions. This is one of the rare cases in the gospels where someone rejects Jesus' invitation to follow him.

The event opens the door for further reflection on discipleship. Jesus shocks his disciples when he declares how hard it is for a person of wealth to enter the kingdom of God. The disciples' shock underlines the common belief of the day that riches and good health were a sign of God's favor. If the rich couldn't enter heaven, who could? Not knowing discipleship demanded sacrifice, the rich young man may have expected Jesus to tell him he could follow him *and* keep his wealth. Mark is again stressing the radical call of discipleship.

Jesus says it's easier for a camel to pass through the eye of a needle than for a rich man to enter the kingdom of heaven. He's saying that it's impossible for a rich man to enter the kingdom of God. But what is impossible with human beings *is* possible with God. Whether a person enters the kingdom of God is totally up to God. Jesus omits the notion of "rich" when he repeats for a second time how hard it is to enter the kingdom of God. Entering the kingdom of God is difficult for everyone, but God makes it possible.

When Peter asks what's in store for those who give up everything to follow him, Jesus gives a solemn answer. Those who have given up much will receive a hundredfold in this world and in the world to come. But,

Jesus adds, they will also be persecuted. This is an important point in the Gospel of Mark, lest the reader think there's no room for persecution in discipleship. Jesus' followers in Mark's day were often rejected or betrayed by their families. Even today, rejection and persecution are endured by those who profess faith in Christ. They're sustained by their belief that their faith will bring them eternal life.

Lectio Divina

Spend 8 to 10 minutes in silent contemplation of the following passage:

> Jesus tells us it's impossible for the rich to enter the reign of God. Often the more wealth we have, the more our wealth possesses us. Peter and the other disciples overcame the trap of wealth. They've left everything to follow Jesus, and they will receive their reward. The challenge of this reading isn't wealth in itself; it's the use of what God has given us. Does it possess us, or do we possess it? Surprisingly, people who have left all to follow Jesus often have happier and more fulfilling lives.

✠ *What can I learn from this passage?*

Day 3: The Prediction of Jesus' Death and Resurrection (10:32–34)

The disciples had been journeying south toward Jerusalem since Peter's profession of faith, but only now does Mark state that Jesus and his disciples are on their way to Jerusalem. Jesus walks in the lead, thus showing members of the early Church that they must follow Jesus to their own passion and resurrection. The disciples, recognizing that Jesus faced danger in Jerusalem, are amazed that Jesus would go near the city. The crowd continues to follow him, but in fear.

For the third time, Jesus predicts his passion, death, and resurrection. The details are more exact in this third prediction: Jesus will be handed over in Jerusalem to the chief priests and the scribes, who will condemn him to death and hand him over to the Gentiles, who will mock him, spit on him, scourge him, and kill him. Mark presents Jesus' journey toward Jerusalem as his messianic journey toward the fulfillment of his mission.

Through his passion, death, and resurrection, Jesus will fulfill his messianic role. As usual, Jesus never speaks of his passion and death without adding a reference to his resurrection. He also predicts that after three days, he will be raised from the dead.

Lectio Divina

Spend 8 to 10 minutes in silent contemplation of the following passage:

> Courage is not acting without fear—it's acting despite fear. Jesus gives us an example of such courage as he heads toward Jerusalem, where he knows he will suffer and die. Jesus knew his fate, but he didn't cringe at the thought of his crucifixion. As we later learn during his agony in the garden, Jesus wasn't immune to fear—he acted despite his fear. As followers of Jesus, we might fear standing up for our faith. The most many of us have to fear is ridicule or rejection for our faith—it's rarely death.

> ✠ *What can I learn from this passage?*

Day 4: Ambition of James and John (10:35–45)

Two disciples, Zebedee's sons James and John, ask Jesus for the seats of honor when he enters his glory, one on his right and the other on his left. Although readers understand the meaning of eternal glory here, the two disciples misunderstand Jesus' mission and believe he's going to establish an earthly kingdom. Jesus warns that they don't know what they're asking and questions whether they can drink of the cup he will drink from or accept the baptism he will receive.

The image of the cup as a reference to suffering is used here and during the passion of Jesus when Jesus begs God to take the cup away from him (14:36). Still misunderstanding, the disciples promptly declare that they *can* drink of this cup and accept a baptism like his. Jesus promises they will indeed receive the cup and baptism of suffering. Jesus then states that the seat at his right or left is not his to give—it belongs to those for whom it has been prepared.

Mark continues to present the Twelve in all their weakness. The other disciples, also misunderstanding Jesus' words, are angry with James and

John. Like James and John, they are ambitious and may have similar desires. Jesus instructs them that the kingdom of God isn't structured in the same manner as pagan kingdoms. The way to greatness in the kingdom of God is through service, not power. Those who wish to be first must be a servant to all. Jesus again speaks of himself as the Son of Man, who will suffer and give his life for others. Mark, in writing for the disciples of his own day, continues to stress the need for service, suffering, persecution, and even death in the call to discipleship. The true disciple doesn't strive for recognition or a place of honor in this world, but for total dedication to Christ and his message.

Lectio Divina

Spend 8 to 10 minutes in silent contemplation of the following passage:

> In serving Christ as a layperson, religious, or clergy, we must replace the temptation to look good before the world with the need to be a good disciple acting in the spirit of the Son of God, who emptied himself to become one with us. People may not see the good we do, but we're not doing it for applause or ambition. Being a disciple means being humbly dedicated to sharing the light of Christ through our way of life. The humble disciple is often the one who has the greatest influence on creation.

✠ *What can I learn from this passage?*

Day 5: The Blind Bartimaeus (10:46–52)

Mark notes that Jesus, his disciples, and a large crowd are leaving Jericho when a blind man named Bartimaeus calls out to Jesus, addressing him by the messianic title of "son of David." This narrative marks another turning point in the Gospel of Mark. Although Bartimaeus is blind, he sees with the eyes of faith that Jesus is the Messiah. Bartimaeus is not as spiritually blind as the disciples of Jesus.

When Bartimaeus repeatedly calls out to Jesus, many rebuke him, but he is rewarded for his persistence: Jesus calls him over. In his enthusiasm to come to Jesus, Bartimaeus abandons the valued possession of a blind man and beggar, his cloak. The cloak kept him warm at night, and during the day people would toss coins onto his cloak. Like a true disciple, he responds immediately when Jesus calls, leaving all else to follow Jesus.

Although it's obvious what Bartimaeus would want, Jesus asks him, "What do you want me to do for you?" Bartimaeus addresses Jesus as "Master," a sign of recognition of Jesus' elite position. Bartimaeus asks for sight, and Jesus cures him. In several passages in Mark's Gospel, Jesus knows what people want, but he makes them ask for it. The message for Jesus' disciples is that God knows our needs, but we must still take the initiative and ask. Faith also plays an important role in the story as Jesus tells Bartimaeus, "Your faith has saved you."

Although Jesus is close to Jerusalem, where we might expect him to keep his identity even more hidden, he no longer gives orders for silence about his messianic role. Mark is telling us that it's time for revelation, a time to begin to recognize Jesus in his messianic role. Mark portrays Bartimaeus as more than just one more healing; he's now a follower of Jesus. The expression "followed him on the way" was used as a call and response of discipleship. This is the only time Mark names the blind man, which implies that Bartimaeus was a well-known follower of Jesus.

Lectio Divina

Spend 8 to 10 minutes in silent contemplation of the following passage:

> The story of Bartimaeus teaches a lesson about prayer and faith. When Jesus passed by, Bartimaeus shouted out with a strong faith, "Jesus, son of David, have pity on me." Jesus may have been testing the blind man's endurance by letting him continue to call out. Finally Jesus asks him what he wants. Although Jesus can see that the man is blind, Jesus makes him ask for healing: "Master, I want to see." Jesus heals him, and Bartimaeus becomes a follower. We learn a lesson about faith and prayer. Bartimaeus shouts out, which is a way of praying, and he persists in his prayer, refusing to stop. Jesus seems indifferent but finally relents. When we pray, God already knows our needs, but God still wants us to ask. We must pray with faith and tell God what we want.

✠ *What can I learn from this passage?*

Review Questions

1. What does Jesus mean when he said we should accept the kingdom of God as a little child would?

2. What does Jesus ask the rich man to do to become a follower?

3. What does Jesus promise those who leave all to follow him?

4. What is significant about Jesus' third prediction of his passion, death, and resurrection?

5. How does Jesus respond to the request of James and John for a place of honor in Jesus' glory?

6. What is significant about the story of Bartimaeus?

Jesus in Jerusalem

MARK 11—13

Therefore I tell you, all that you ask for in prayer, believe that you will receive it and it shall be yours. (11:24)

Opening Prayer (SEE PAGE 18)

Context

Part 1: Mark 11—12:12 The author presents Jesus' conflict with religious leaders. Jesus enters Jerusalem to the praise of a crowd shouting "Hosanna in the highest." The next day Jesus, who is hungry, strangely curses a fig tree for not bearing fruit even though it's not fig season. After that, he enters the Temple and casts out the merchants, showing anger because they've made God's house into a marketplace. The next morning Peter is shocked to discover that the fig tree has withered, and Jesus uses the occasion to teach that a person of great faith can perform great miracles. When Jesus enters the Temple, the religious leaders demand to know the source of Jesus' supposed authority. When they refuse to answer Jesus' question concerning the authority of John the Baptist, Jesus refuses to answer their question, realizing that they're not capable of accepting the true answer about the source of his authority. Jesus alienates the religious leaders even further by relating a parable about unjust vineyard tenants who kill those sent by the owner to collect payment. The leaders realize Jesus is implying that *they* are the unjust servants.

Part 2: Mark 12:13—13 Jesus answers a series of questions concerning the payment of taxes to Rome, the resurrection from the dead, and the greatest commandment. He asks the scribes about David's calling the Messiah his Lord even though David was clearly an early ancestor of the Messiah and therefore believed to be greater. Jesus warns the people against the example of the scribes, who seek praise for their religious actions. Jesus praises a widow who has given a small amount to the Temple treasury, declaring that she has given more than all the rest because she gave out of her need, not out of her surplus.

As Jesus leaves, he speaks about the Temple's destruction. He tells his disciples that the end is not near when they hear of total annihilation of the world through wars or earthquakes. He also warns the disciples that they'll be betrayed even by family members because of their faith. He warns of a great destruction, a reference to the destruction of Jerusalem. When this happens, they will need to flee immediately, turning back for nothing. False messiahs and prophets will appear and mislead many.

Jesus turns his attention to the end of the world, speaking of great catastrophes in the heavens and of angels coming to gather the just from all over the world. Although the people can read the signs of the seasons, they must also see the signs of the end. They are to be as alert as servants awaiting a master's return from a trip.

PART 1: GROUP STUDY (MARK 11—12:12)

Read aloud Mark 11—12:12.

11:1–11 Jesus' Triumphal Entry Into Jerusalem

Jesus draws near to Jerusalem at the Mount of Olives. Zechariah, an Old Testament prophet, speaks of the Lord's beginning his war against the nations by plundering Jerusalem and resting his feet on the Mount of Olives (14:4). Many Jews believed that salvation would originate on the Mount of Olives. As he does in preparation for the Passover meal, Jesus takes the initiative and sends two of his disciples into the village, where they'll find a tethered colt no one has ever ridden. That image fits the Jewish description of an animal prepared for a religious ceremony. Although Mark offers no hint of previous preparation by Jesus and his disciples, the bystanders allow the disciples to take the colt at the mention of the Master's need. Jesus promises to return the colt immediately after using it.

Jesus enters Jerusalem seated on the colt as foretold by Zechariah, who wrote, "Behold: your king is coming to you, a just savior is he, Humble, and riding on a donkey, on a colt, the foal of a donkey" (9:9). The feast seems to be the Jewish Feast of Tabernacles, when people carried reeds and palms in procession. The idea of laying cloaks on the back of the colt and along the road shows the royal homage people pay to Jesus. The praise offered to Jesus comes from Psalm 118:26, which proclaims "Blessed is he who comes in the name of the LORD," and which was sung during the Feast of Tabernacles.

During the feast, people would pray a prayer that came to be known as *Hoshanos,* which became "Hosanna" in many current translations. The people would use this prayer during Jesus' triumphal entry into Jerusalem. It's originally a prayer for God's blessing, with each phrase of the prayer ending with the word *hoshana,* "please save" or "save now!" Although the people praise Jesus as the prophet of the messianic kingdom, they don't proclaim him the Messiah. They declare that he comes in the name of the Lord, which means he comes with the Lord's authority. This question of authority will become the center of Jesus' first confrontation in Jerusalem.

Mark doesn't present this entry in Jerusalem in the glorious and elaborate manner of the Gospels of Matthew, Luke, or John. The crowd seems to be small, and no mention is made that others take notice of the crowd. They connect Jesus with the kingdom of David to come.

The Feast of the Tabernacles centered on the Temple. It's significant that Mark ends this passage with Jesus' brief inspection of the Temple area. This lays the groundwork for the cleansing of the Temple. Since it's late, nothing happens on this first inspection. He goes to Bethany with his disciples.

11:12–19 Jesus Cleanses the Temple

Mark's Gospel presents a short passage about Jesus and a barren fig tree, which becomes a parable in action. Mark uses the story to frame another episode with a similar message. When Jesus and the Twelve pass the fig tree, Jesus curses it for not bearing fruit even though it isn't fig season. Mark then turns his attention to Jesus' cleansing of the Temple, but he will return to the story of the fig tree as they leave the Temple. Mark sandwiches the story of the Temple into his story of the fig tree to show the stories in relation to each other. Hosea, an Old Testament prophet, compares Israel to a fig tree that doesn't bear good fruit (9:10). Jesus' disciples hear him curse the tree, stating that no one will eat its fruit again. The episodes foreshadow the end of the Temple, which occurs later in history.

People who came to the Temple for the feast would buy animals for sacrifice just inside the Temple precincts. They would also trade their Greek and Roman coins, which were considered unclean for temple exchange, for temple coins. Suddenly Jesus disrupts this practice, overturning the tables of the money changers and the seats of those selling doves and not allowing anyone to carry anything into the Temple area. Exchanging coins and selling doves were allowed in the outermost court of the Temple, the area of the Gentiles, where the merchants sold doves for sacrifices the poor offered in place of the more expensive offerings. Mark makes a point that is important to his Gentile readers: The house of God is for all people, not only for Jews. Jesus' anger seems to stem not only from the sinful cheating within the Temple precincts, but also because even though the Temple was for all people, many Jewish leaders restricted some areas to Jews. Jesus' act of authority in the Temple was replacing the authority of the religious leaders who, until that time, had sole authority over the use of the Temple.

When the chief priests and scribes hear of Jesus' rage in the Temple and his challenge to their authority, they seek to destroy him, but they fear him because the crowd is amazed at his teaching. By stressing that the religious leaders' resentment is building against Jesus, Mark prepares his readers for Jesus' passion and death.

That evening Jesus and his companions leave the city, and when they return in the morning the astonished disciples see the fig tree withered to its roots. The withered fig tree is a symbol of Israel and the Temple. Because they haven't borne the fruit they existed to bear, they are cursed and will wither. The situation foreshadows the day in the year 70 when the Romans invade Jerusalem and destroy the city and the Temple.

11:20–26 The Power of Faithful Prayer

Mark changes the message of the barren fig tree into a message of the power of faith and prayer. When the amazed disciples ask Jesus how the fig tree withered so quickly, Jesus tells them that if they have unwavering faith, they will be able to perform great and even impossible actions, even to the point of commanding mountains to cast themselves into the sea or uprooting trees. Jesus isn't urging the Twelve to use their gifts in a frivolous manner such as physically moving mountains; he uses this imagery to express the great power of faith and prayer. People of faith perform spiritual deeds that seem impossible. Jesus urges his listeners to trust the power of prayer. What they ask for with faith, they receive. True prayer consists not only of word but also attitude, in this case an attitude of forgiveness. People who forgive allow God to in turn forgive them and answer their prayer. As he does often in the gospels, Jesus connects our forgiveness of others with the power of prayer.

11:27–33 Questioning Jesus' Authority

Jesus' activities in the Temple naturally lead to conflict with the leaders. Since the religious leaders had authority in the Temple, they challenge Jesus' action of authority. Mark follows this episode with five conflict stories. Temple leaders realize that any authority greater than theirs must come from God, but they don't believe Jesus' authority comes from God. Mark names three groups who approach Jesus in the Temple precincts: the chief priests, the scribes, and the elders. Members of each group formed the Sanhedrin, a major group within Judaism that would later decide Jesus' fate. Unafraid of being confronted about his rage in the Temple, Jesus returns to Jerusalem and is walking in the Temple area when the religious leaders question him about his authority.

Mark presents this first conflict in the form of a true rabbinical debate, in which one question is answered with another to force opponents to reach certain clear conclusions. When the leaders ask Jesus about the source of his authority, they're really asking whether he believes his authority truly comes from God. Jesus responds with a question about John the Baptist's baptism: Did John's baptism come from God or from some human source? Jesus promises that if the religious leaders answer his question sincerely, he'll answer theirs.

The Jewish leaders can't answer Jesus' question without trapping themselves. To declare that John's authority came from God would be to condemn themselves because they rejected John. To declare that the authority came from a human source would put the Jewish leaders in conflict with the crowd, who consider John a true prophet. Their inability to answer the question shows that they're unable to understand any answer Jesus could give. If Jesus says his authority comes from God, they will have as difficult a time accepting it as they did accepting John's authority. Jesus, therefore, refuses to answer their question.

Mark is indirectly presenting a pronouncement story: The source of Jesus' authority is the source of John's authority. The members of the early Church knew John's authority came from God. Mark's readers would have to smile at the manner in which Jesus turned the question of authority against his opponents.

12:1–12 Parable of the Tenants

In the second conflict story, Jesus presents a parable to Jewish leaders. Because the parable has become an allegory that gives specific meaning to many parts of the story, we can conclude that it evolved as it was preached in the early Church community. In the parable, a vineyard symbolizes the reign of God and tenant farmers symbolize the Jewish leaders. The owner of the vineyard, God, sends the prophets into the vineyard to collect God's due. Throughout Old Testament history, the prophets God sent into the vineyard of Israel were beaten, abused, and killed by the leaders. The tenant farmers wish to keep the vineyard for themselves, so they kill the son. They drag him outside the vineyard, a symbol of not giving him a proper burial. As a result of the tenant farmers' rejection of the son, the vineyard is taken away and turned over to others. The members of the early Church community for whom Mark is writing recognize these other farmers as the Gentiles.

Jesus changes the image from a vineyard to a building and, quoting Psalm 118:22–23, he declares that those who have rejected him are actually rejecting the cornerstone (keystone) of the structure, the part on which the total structure depends. If the keystone is removed, the whole structure collapses. Mark remarks that the leaders recognized themselves in this parable as the tenant farmers, and they would have arrested Jesus immediately if they hadn't feared the crowd's reaction. Instead, they depart without arresting him.

Review Questions

1. What is significant about Jesus' entry into Jerusalem?
2. Why does Jesus drive the money changers and dove sellers out of the Temple?
3. What is the significance of the withered fig tree?
4. Why are the scribes and elders indignant because Jesus turns over the tables of the money changers and the seats of the dove sellers?
5. How does Jesus respond to the scribes and elders when they challenge his authority?
6. What does the parable of the tenants say about the religious leaders of Jesus' day and about us today?

Closing Prayer (SEE PAGE 18)

Pray the closing prayer now or after *lectio divina*.

Lectio Divina (SEE PAGE 11)

Relax your body and maintain a posture of prayer (back straight, eyes shut, feet flat on the floor). This exercise can take as long as you want, but in the context of this Bible study, 10 to 20 minutes should be sufficient.

The meditations that follow are provided only to help group participants use this prayer form, but note that *lectio* is intended to bring one to a place of prayerful contemplation where the Word of God speaks to the hearer from his or her heart. (See page 11 for further instruction.)

Jesus Triumphal Entry Into Jerusalem (11:1–11)

In our prayer, God blesses us with consolation, sometimes to strengthen us for difficulties ahead or simply to remind us that God is present when we pray. God may give us our Palm Sundays before our Good Fridays as a means of supporting us during our struggles. We're able to endure all tragedies because Good Fridays are followed by Easter Sundays. Life is filled with many minor deaths and resurrections until the moment we enter eternity and share in our final and most glorious resurrection. Throughout our journey of life to resurrection, Christ is with us.

✠ *What can I learn from this passage?*

Jesus Cleanses the Temple (11:12–19)

Jesus' rage against those selling merchandise in the Temple has nothing to do with selling religious articles in the gathering areas of church buildings today, where people meet to prepare for worship before they move into the worship area. Like the innermost areas of the Temple, the worship area is sacred and open to everyone no matter their faith, spiritual condition, or social class. Sinners and saints are welcome. The worship area is a sacred space set apart for an assembly to worship in as the loving community of the Body of Christ.

✠ *What can I learn from this passage?*

The Power of Faithful Prayer (11:20–26)

Jesus again stresses the need for faith in prayer. Faith enables us to seek miracles, and prayer with faith can be powerful enough to lead God to perform miracles. We may not immediately perceive the results of our prayers, but Jesus calls us to pray with unwavering faith and trust that God is answering our prayer in some manner, no matter how impossible the answer may seem. "Lord, I do believe, help my unbelief."

✠ *What can I learn from this passage?*

Questioning Jesus' Authority (11:27–33)

Christians recognize that Jesus' authority comes from God just as John's baptismal mission does. Although we can answer Jesus' question, we must also ask how much of Jesus' message touches us. If we really believe Jesus' authority comes from God, then our lives must reflect Jesus' life. Some people have *notional* faith: They profess their belief, but their way of life and their values contradict their statements. Actual faith occurs when we base our actions on Jesus' life and message. Jesus asks us to have true faith—to be a living example of our faith.

✠ *What can I learn from this passage?*

Parable of the Tenants (12:1–12)

Followers of Christ become the tenant farmers, whose duty it is to bring forth a harvest for God. Ambition, pride, or a desire to reject Christ and not use his gifts can lead to eviction from God's vineyard. That message applies even today to all Christians who have the privilege of faith but who must remain faithful to the master of the vineyard, God. Complacency has no place in following Jesus, the cornerstone of our faith. God sent the Son into the vineyard, and we must decide how we'll respond to this great gift of the Son of God in our midst.

✠ *What can I learn from this passage?*

PART 2: INDIVIDUAL STUDY (MARK 12:13—13)

Day 1: Question About Paying Taxes (12:13–17)

In this third conflict story, the Pharisees and the Herodians join forces to confront Jesus about taxes paid to a foreign ruler. The Herodians supported the tax, while some Pharisees sought to pay the taxes to keep peace. Many people, resentful of foreign domination, believed no tax should be paid to a foreign ruler. The clever question was meant to trap Jesus. If he agreed with the tax, people would turn against him as one who supported foreign domination. If he rejected the tax, he could be turned over to the Roman authorities as one who publicly refused to pay the tax. In posing the question, the Herodians and Pharisees exhibit their hypocrisy in first praising Jesus as a truthful man dedicated to teaching the way of God in accordance with that truth. Jesus, as usual, sees through their hypocrisy and asks why they continue to test him. In answer to their question, he asks for a *denarius*, a Roman coin.

The Jews believed a person owned anything that carried that person's image. Jesus again answers a question with a question. He asks them whose image is on the coin, and they answer that it is Caesar. The coin must therefore belong to Caesar. Creation, which carries the image of God, belongs to God, so must people worship God above all else in creation. Jesus makes a pronouncement at the end when he tells the people to give to the emperor what belongs to the emperor, and to give to God what belongs to God. What the emperor receives is nothing compared to the worship owed to God. The shrewdness of Jesus' answer leaves the crowds amazed.

The answer also helps Mark's audience, who must face the same question. Should they pay taxes to pagan rulers? In the early Church, it was important that Christians become good, faithful citizens to avoid unnecessary persecution. They must accept persecution for their faith, but not for refusing to follow laws of the land that didn't infringe on their beliefs. Jesus' message has implications today in understanding the roles of state and church.

Lectio Divina

Spend 8 to 10 minutes in silent contemplation of the following passage:

> Being a good citizen in a just society is a central message of Catholic teaching. Catholics have an obligation to fulfill their civic functions in the best way. Jesus led by example, saying we should balance our citizenship and faith by rendering to the state (government) what belongs to the state and to God what belongs to God. Jesus points out that because the coin bears the Caesar's image, it belongs to Caesar. According to the creation story, human beings bear God's image. We have the power to think, judge, act, and offer our lives to God. We can ask ourselves if our actions as a citizen conform to our image of God.

✠ *What can I learn from this passage?*

Day 2: The Question About Resurrection (12:18–27)

The Sadducees, for the only time in the Gospel of Mark, challenge Jesus. The Sadducees refuse to believe in resurrection of the dead because they accept only the first five books of the Bible (known as the *Torah*), none of which mention resurrection. The Pharisees, who accept other books as part of the authentic Scriptures, support the idea of resurrection from the dead. The Sadducees confront Jesus, pointing to a Law of Moses in the Book of Deuteronomy, one of the first five books of the Bible, in which Moses taught that a man must marry his brother's wife if his brother dies without a male heir (25:5–10). The people of ancient Israel believed a person's spirit was immortal because it continued in the male heir and carried on through the family name. Lack of a male heir would lead to the tragic end of immortality. The first male child born of a union between a brother and his sister-in-law was considered a child of the dead brother, giving the dead brother a second chance at immortality.

The Sadducees ask Jesus whose wife a woman will be at the time of resurrection if she marries seven brothers who die without male heirs. Jesus again responds with a question, asking whether they're misled because they don't know Scripture or the power of God. The Sadducees, who pride themselves on their knowledge of Scripture, are insulted by Jesus' question.

Jesus offers two answers to the question. He first tells the Sadducees that they misunderstand the whole idea of resurrection. It isn't a continuation of this life, but a new type of existence equivalent to their understanding of the existence of the angels. Marriage doesn't exist in this new type of existence; however, Jesus does not say that people won't recognize their spouses.

Jesus' second answer comes from an Old Testament quotation from the Book of Exodus, one of the first five books of the Bible and therefore accepted by the Sadducees. God appeared to Moses in the burning bush and said, "I am the God of your father,...the God of Abraham, the God of Isaac, and the God of Jacob" (3:6). God is a God of the living and not the dead; therefore Abraham, Isaac, and Jacob, although dead to this world, must be among the living. God didn't say, "I was"—God said "I am" the God of these patriarchs, as though they still existed. These words of God, taken from the Scripture, imply a resurrection.

At the time Mark wrote his gospel, Christians believed in resurrection not only because of Jesus' words, but also because of their faith in Jesus' actual resurrection. For people enduring persecution and even death, Mark's reminder about Jesus' teachings on resurrection offers encouragement.

Lectio Divina

Spend 8 to 10 minutes in silent contemplation of the following passage:

Resurrection is the great hope of Christianity. We hope to rise one day in union with Christ. Jesus teaches that people do rise into eternal life. When someone we love dies, we believe that person is living in a different manner in eternity—in eternal glory, we hope. Although we believe the deceased person is alive in eternity, we nevertheless grieve: "I have you, but I don't have you as I had you." Faith in Jesus leads to faith in resurrection.

✠ *What can I learn from this passage?*

Day 3: The Greatest Commandment (12:28–34)

A scribe, impressed with Jesus' answers to his opponents, asks Jesus a question commonly debated among the rabbis of Jesus' day. But unlike the other religious leaders, the scribe is sincerely trying to learn. The past debates attempted to get all of God's commandments into as short a statement as possible so they could determine the one commandment that contained all the others. The scribe asks Jesus which commandment is the greatest. Since the scribe approaches Jesus in an honest and friendly manner and not as an adversary, Jesus doesn't answer his question with a question.

Jesus answers with a quotation from a prayer the Israelites prayed twice a day, "The Lord our God is Lord alone!," and adds the command to love God with one's heart, soul, mind, and strength. Jesus then speaks of a second commandment equal to the first, namely that we should love our neighbor as ourself. He ends by stating that no commandment is greater than these.

The answer actually joins two quotations from the Old Testament, the first concerning love of God (see Deuteronomy 6:5) and the second concerning love of one's neighbor (see Leviticus 19:18). The apparent value of Jesus' answer is that he places these two commandments together. These commands, found in the middle of the passage, are the statements toward which this pronouncement story points.

The scribe agrees with Jesus' answer, implying that the scribe accepts the answer as a commandment to be lived in his own life. Jesus tells the scribe he isn't far from the kingdom of God. The passage ends with the leaders finally recognizing Jesus' wisdom and skill in the debate, and no one has the courage to ask Jesus more questions.

When Mark's audience read Jesus' words, they recognized the difficulty in being Jesus' follower. Mark's audience suffered at the hands of persecutors and recognized that somehow they need to learn to love those who persecuted them. Jesus offers not only words—he shows love for his persecutors even as he later faces his passion and death. Jesus is the ultimate example of love of God and neighbor.

Lectio Divina

Spend 8 to 10 minutes in silent contemplation of the following passage:

> The centerpiece of Jesus' teaching is to love God with all our heart, soul, mind, and strength and to love our neighbor as ourselves. Love of God naturally demands love of neighbor. The author of John's first letter writes, "If anyone says, 'I love God,' but hates his brother, he is a liar" (1 John 4:20). Love of one's neighbor puts into practice our love of God. This demands availability and concern for our neighbor even when it's most inconvenient or challenging, such as when we need to forgive. The final command demands love of self, which we show when we avoid becoming selfish. Selfishness can cause us to become proud and arrogant, less like Jesus and thus less loving of ourself.

✠ *What can I learn from this passage?*

_____

Day 4: The Questions About David's Son (12:35–44)

Jesus now poses his own question. In Jewish thought, a male ancestor was considered to be greater than his offspring. Jesus draws on this belief when he speaks of a psalm believed by the people of Jesus' day to have been written by David. However, David wasn't the author of that psalm. Psalm 110:1 has David referring to one of his offspring as "Lord." If David was greater than any of his offspring, he would never have addressed that person with a title that put that offspring above him. Jesus challenges the scribes to explain how David could address one of his offspring as "Lord." The scribes expected a messiah who would come from the Davidic line, but they didn't expect a divine messiah. Because of this, they are unable to answer Jesus' question.

Jesus warns his listeners against the display of honor shown by the scribes who pray lengthy prayers and devour the houses of widows. Luke links the word *widow* in the previous section with Jesus' words of praise for the actions of a widow who contributes to the Temple treasury out of her need rather than from her surplus wealth.

Lectio Divina

Spend 8 to 10 minutes in silent contemplation of the following passage:

> David, as great as he is in Israel's history, must still bow down to Jesus
> as Lord. No one could have dreamed that the Messiah would also be
> God. Even now, long after the event, we should still be amazed that
> the Son of God actually became flesh and dwelt among us.

✠ *What can I learn from this passage?*

Day 5: The Arrival of the End (13)

One of Jesus' disciples speaks in awe of the Temple structure, but Jesus
responds that everything will be torn down and destroyed. He warns
his disciples that false prophets will arise at the time of the destruction
of Jerusalem and the Temple. In the early Church, many believed that
the end was soon to come. Jesus points out that war and rumor of war
don't necessarily mean the end is near. The apocalyptic image of war,
earthquakes, and famine shouldn't be construed as an announcement
that the last days have arrived. Christians will find themselves persecuted at the hands of foreign governments, synagogue leaders, and their
own families. The Holy Spirit will give them the courage needed in such
a time of persecution.

Jesus speaks of a sacrilegious and destructive presence that recalls
the words of Daniel, the prophet, who spoke of "desolating abomination"
(9:27) as a reference to the pagan altar that Antiochus IV constructed in
the Temple around 168 BC. The invasion of Rome will be so swift that the
inhabitants won't have time to turn back for their possessions. Despite the
power of the Roman army, God will intervene for the sake of those who
pray, shortening the days of destruction and suffering.

In highly symbolic and apocalyptic language, Jesus announces the second
coming or, as it is also called, the *Parousia*. The apocalyptic literature speaks
of signs in the skies such as darkness in place of the sun and moon, stars
falling from the skies, and all the heavens trembling. In the midst of this
will come the glorious Son of Man, Jesus Christ, riding on the clouds in
all his heavenly glory and power. The angels will go out to the four winds,

which symbolize the four ends of the Earth. All the chosen from Earth and sky will be assembled for the day of glorious triumph.

Just as people can read the change of seasons in a simple fig tree, so should they learn the end is near when they see all the events of Jesus' final discourse being fulfilled. The Son doesn't know when these events will take place.

Jesus delivers a short parable about a man who leaves others in charge of his home as he travels. The servants don't know when he will return, so they must always be prepared. It wouldn't be a good day for a servant who was asleep when his master returned. In the same way, we too should be constantly awake and watchful for the sudden return of Jesus.

Lectio Divina

Spend 8 to 10 minutes in silent contemplation of the following passage:

A constant theme in Scripture is that we should always be prepared when the Lord calls us. Although Jesus speaks about the End Times, we must realize that the end time for each of us is when God calls us from this life or when the world ends. In either case, we must always be watchful, alert, and faithful to God.

✠ *What can I learn from this passage?*

Review Questions

1. How does Jesus answer those who asked whether he pays taxes to Caesar?

2. How does Jesus answer the Sadducees when they challenge him about resurrection?

3. Which does Jesus say is the greatest commandment? Why?

4. How does Jesus respond to those who believe David wrote the psalm proclaiming one of his offspring as Lord and therefore apparently greater than David?

LESSON 8

Jesus' Passion and Resurrection

MARK 14–16

When the centurion who stood facing him saw how he breathed his last he said, 'Truly this man was the Son of God. (15:39)

Opening Prayer (SEE PAGE 18)

Context

Note: *In this lesson, Part 1 takes place scripturally after Part 2 because the passages in Part 1 are more appropriate for group study.*

Part 1: Mark 15:21—16 Jesus is crucified and mocked while on the cross. When he dies, the veil of the sanctuary in the Temple is torn in two, a sign of the end of temple worship. A centurion proclaims Jesus as the Son of God. Some women witness Jesus' burial. On the first day of the week, three women find the tomb empty and receive the news that Jesus has been raised. They leave, telling no one.

In the longer edition about the resurrection added to Mark's Gospel, Jesus appears to Mary Magdalen, who tells Jesus' disciples he is alive. Jesus appears to two of his disciples walking on their way to the country. Jesus later appears to the disciples, rebukes them for their lack of faith, and gives them the mission of spreading the gospel to every creature. They receive power to perform great works in Jesus' name. Jesus ascends in the sight of the disciples, and the disciples become witnesses to Jesus.

Part 2: Mark 14—15:20 The religious leaders plot to arrest Jesus and put him to death, but they suspect that arresting Jesus would cause a riot. In the meantime, a woman anoints Jesus' head with expensive oil; and some in the group are furious, saying the sale of the oil would have brought money for the poor. Jesus proclaims that the woman has anointed him for his burial. Judas plots to hand Jesus over to the religious leaders. Jesus' disciples prepare the Passover meal, at which Jesus predicts that one of them will betray him and warns about the horrible torment the betrayer will face.

At the Last Supper, Jesus gives the bread and wine to his disciples, saying that these are his Body and Blood. Peter bravely boasts that he will die with Christ, but Jesus predicts that Peter will deny him three times. Jesus and the disciples go to Gethsemane, where he endures his agony in the garden. He prays that his coming passion would bypass him, but he abandons himself to the Father's will. Judas points Jesus out to an armed crowd. Jesus is brought before the Sanhedrin, where he's judged worthy of death. Peter, in the meantime, denies Jesus three times and, repenting, breaks down in tears. Jesus receives a death sentence. The soldiers mock Jesus as a king, place a crown of thorns on his head, and lead him to his crucifixion.

PART 1: GROUP STUDY (MARK 15:21—16)

Read aloud Mark 15:21—16.

15:21–32 The Crucifixion of Jesus

A condemned person in Jesus' day would ordinarily carry a beam used for the cross across his outstretched arms and shoulders. Possibly because of Jesus' weakened condition, the soldiers force a man named Simon, from the land of Cyrene, to carry Jesus' cross. Mark mentions that Simon is the father of Alexander and Rufus, which implies that his sons are well known to the early Church community.

The place of crucifixion is Golgotha, or "the place of a skull," a name that describes the appearance of the hill where the crucifixion takes place. The only mercy shown a condemned person was to allow him to drink a light drug. Jesus, fully accepting his suffering to the end, refuses the drink.

The condemned person's clothing was customarily divided among the soldiers, and Psalm 22:19 speaks of soldiers casting lots for the garments of the condemned suffering servant. Mark gives the time of the crucifixion as 9:00 AM. The reason for execution was usually placed on a plaque above the head of the crucified. The irony of the crucifixion continues as the inscription above Jesus' head proclaims him "The King of the Jews."

All four gospels speak of two criminals being crucified with Jesus, thus fulfilling the prophecy of Isaiah, who foretold that Jesus would be "counted among the transgressors" (53:12). The place of crucifixion was near a well-traveled road where passersby could see what happened to criminals condemned by Roman authority.

The crowd's mockery contains many details that would be recognized by the early Church community. In response to those who laughed at Jesus because he claimed he would rebuild the Temple in three days, early Church members realized that Jesus would indeed be raised up in three days as the living Temple of the New Israel.

In response to those who called for Jesus to come down from the cross to save himself, early Church members realized that by remaining on the cross, Jesus saved all people. Religious leaders mockingly address Jesus as the Messiah, the King of Israel. Mark has most likely placed this title on the lips of the jeering people, yet it reminds the reader that precisely by remaining on the cross can Jesus claim these titles. Mark notes that both criminals taunt Jesus.

15:33–41 Jesus Dies on the Cross

The power of evil dominates as Mark describes the darkness that covers the Earth from noon till 3:00 PM. From the cross, Jesus cries out, "My God, my God, why have you forsaken me?" Some commentators say Jesus is reciting the first lines of Psalm 22 ("My God, my God, why have you abandoned me?"), which ends on a note of triumph by declaring that generations to come will be told of the Lord's deliverance. Others commentators claim that Jesus is expressing his deep feeling of desolation and abandonment by everyone, including God. For them, Jesus is expressing his experience of painful loneliness on the cross. In Mark's Gospel, Jesus is totally abandoned and alone, with no one nearby to comfort him.

Ancient Jewish folklore held that Elijah would come to release prisoners from foreign powers, and some bystanders misinterpret Jesus' cry as a cry for Elijah's help. One bystander offers Jesus a mixture of sour wine that was thought to alleviate pain, although Mark implies that this was given as part of the crowd's mockery. The person giving the wine said they should wait to see if Elijah came before taking Jesus down from the cross.

Like the people throughout the Gospel of Mark who give up their spirits at the moment of exorcism with a loud cry, Jesus lets out a loud cry and breathes his last. Although we must wait for Jesus' resurrection to understand his full triumph over the powers of evil, some of the visible effects are immediate. Even at the moment of his death, Jesus has triumphed. The Temple curtain is torn in two, marking the end of the old covenant. A centurion proclaims words of triumph at Jesus' death when he understands the whole meaning of Jesus' ministry and declares, "Truly this man was the Son of God!" The centurion's words bring the reader back to the beginning of Mark's Gospel, where Mark proclaims he is writing about Jesus Christ, *the Son of God.*

In Mark's Gospel, the women remained at a distance, faithful to Jesus but never receiving recognition until this moment. Mary Magdalene, Mary the mother of James and John, and Salome, who are named, were apparently well known to the early Church. That they stand in the distance recalls Psalm 38:12, in which a sinner speaks of his friends' standing in the distance because of his afflictions. These women tended to Jesus' needs in Galilee, where he was well received, and they followed him to Jerusalem. That these women came from Galilee and not from Jerusalem signifies that Jesus wasn't treated well in Jerusalem. Mark notes that many other women had come with him to Jerusalem. According to custom, gospel writers say little about the women supporting Jesus, although many women apparently traveled with Jesus and his disciples.

15:42–47 Jesus' Burial

Although the Sanhedrin had passed sentence on Jesus and brought him to Pilate to be crucified, Sanhedrin member Joseph of Arimathea makes a courageous request of Pilate. He wants to bury Jesus' body to show that not all members of the Sanhedrin agreed with the verdict against Jesus. The Romans usually left a victim's body on the cross to decay and be eaten by scavenger birds. They had eased this practice due to Jewish sensitivities concerning the sacredness of the body. When Joseph asks for Jesus' body, Pilate asks a centurion whether Jesus has died. Mark has a centurion make this verification rather than one of Jesus' disciples to stress that Jesus was truly deceased. Pilate, surprised Jesus died so quickly, releases the body to Joseph. Mark alone mentions that Jesus is wrapped in a newly bought linen cloth. Two women, Mary Magdalene and Mary the mother of Joses, are listed as witnesses to Jesus' hasty burial in a new tomb recently hewn out of the rock, and a stone is rolled across the tomb entrance. The reason for the haste and the lack of burial preparation is that the Sabbath was about to begin, and burial rites were not allowed on the Sabbath.

16:1–8 Jesus Is Raised

Mark is precise about the time the three women who followed Jesus' crucifixion at a distance come to the tomb. It's the first day of the week, the day after the Sabbath, just after sunrise. That they would want to anoint a body that had already been in the tomb for so long seems strange, as does their not wondering about the heavy stone covering the tomb's entrance until they're already on their journey. When the women find the stone already rolled back, they're amazed as they encounter a young man (an angel) inside the tomb in a white robe. The white robe signifies a heavenly visitation.

The angel, knowing the women seek Jesus of Nazareth, interprets the message of the empty tomb. The angel invites them to look at the spot where Jesus was laid and tells them Jesus has been raised. The phrase "has been raised" refers to the image that Jesus didn't rise on his own, but that God the Father has raised him.

The use of the title "Jesus of Nazareth" by the angel links the risen Jesus with the historical Jesus: This Jesus is the same one who lived, suffered, and died. The angel also refers to him as the "crucified," which further links the resurrected Jesus with the historical Jesus. The angel tells the women that Jesus is going ahead of them to Galilee as he foretold. The image of Galilee shouldn't be seen as the land of Galilee alone, but as a theological foundation where Jesus would lead his disciples into the world and where Jesus' followers would experience him in his Second Coming.

The angel directs the women to bring the news about Jesus to the disciples and Peter. The explicit naming of Peter shows the place of prominence Peter held in the early Church. The women, filled with reverential awe and fear, flee from the tomb and say "nothing to anyone." They're left wondering about the message of the empty tomb.

At this point, Mark ends his gospel. The ending leaves us hanging, waiting for something more, but it's fitting that Mark ends his gospel here because he's looking toward the Second Coming of Christ. For Mark, the resurrection has taken place, and the total fulfillment of Christ's mission will come with the Second Coming.

16:9–20 The Resurrected Jesus and His Followers (Long Ending)

From death to life! Commentators have referred to Mark's Gospel as a passion story with a long introduction. Everything in Mark leads to Jesus' death, and at the end he presents the resurrection as a final triumph over evil.

The abruptness of this gospel's ending was apparently unacceptable to a later writer, who added the longer ending, drawing much of its tradition from the other three gospels as well as from the Acts of the Apostles. The author of this section introduces Mary Magdalene as though she is being mentioned for the first time. She's described as the woman who had seven demons cast out of her (Luke 8:2), the one chosen to bring the news of the risen Jesus to the unbelieving disciples (Luke 24:10–11; John 20:11–18). This episode and the next passage—about the two men who receive a revelation about the risen Jesus—come from the Gospel of Luke (24:13–35). The central message is brought out again as the disciples refuse to accept the witness of these two disciples. They must see for themselves.

Finally, as found in all the other gospels, Jesus appears to the Eleven. He berates them for not accepting the words of the witnesses sent ahead to proclaim his resurrection. Jesus then sends the Eleven forth to proclaim the Good News to the world. Jesus recalls for them the signs of God's presence, such as handling serpents, drinking deadly poison without harm, and healing the sick. The author of this part of the gospel doesn't expect his readers to go out and perform these actions; they shouldn't be taken literally. Jesus' ascension recalls the event as portrayed by Luke in his gospel (24:50–53) and in Acts of the Apostles (1:9). The author of this addition to the Gospel of Mark is now satisfied that the message of Jesus' resurrection and ascension has been told in full.

The Mission of Salvation (Short Ending)

The short ending of Mark's Gospel, although not written by Mark, follows verse 8. Like the preceding long ending, this short ending is found in some later Greek manuscripts of the gospel. The women go to Peter and the disciples and send through them the sacred and perpetual proclamation of eternal salvation throughout the world (from East to West). This portion of the gospel is written like a long prayer, as he ends with "Amen."

Review Questions

1. Why do the soldiers mock Jesus?

2. Why do so many people jeer at and ridicule Jesus while he is on the cross?

3. What happens when Jesus dies?

4. What are the significant points of Jesus' burial?

5. How do the women who come to Jesus' tomb on Sunday morning learn of his resurrection?

6. What does the angel tell the women to do?

7. What happens when Mary Magdalene tells Jesus' companions that he is raised?

8. What does Jesus say to the Eleven when he sends them out to preach to all nations?

9. What do unknown authors add to the Gospel of Mark?

Closing Prayer (SEE PAGE 18)

Pray the closing prayer now or after *lectio divina.*

Lectio Divina (SEE PAGE 11)

Relax your body and maintain a posture of prayer (back straight, eyes shut, feet flat on the floor). This exercise can take as long as you want, but in the context of this Bible study, 10 to 20 minutes should be sufficient.

The meditations that follow are provided only to help group participants use this prayer form, but note that *lectio* is intended to bring one to a place of prayerful contemplation where the Word of God speaks to the hearer from his or her heart. (See page 11 for further instruction.)

The Crucifixion of Jesus (15:21–32)

Jesus' crucifixion has inspired Christians throughout the ages to offer their lives for others. Jesus, the Son of God, endured the agonizing journey to the crucifixion, accepting the nails, the mockery, and the ignominy of being crucified as a criminal for the sake of sinful people. Martyrs throughout the centuries have died remembering all Christ endured. Like Jesus, many of them willingly accepted a mission that would inevitably lead to death. Others accepted a mission that wouldn't necessarily lead to death, but that could easily lead to ridicule and suffering. Jesus' crucifixion gave them strength to endure their call from God.

✠ *What can I learn from this passage?*

Jesus Dies on the Cross (15:33–41)

In the early Church, many pagans admired the courage of those who could stare death firmly in the face in the Roman arena, sometimes even rejoicing that they had been chosen to die for Christ. Some pagans knew that the inspiration for those willing to die came from faith in Jesus who, they believed, died on the cross for love of them. The pagans' admiration for the martyrs led to many conversions. The light of Christ shone through their manner of death. Others in the early Church didn't have to face death, but they willingly professed their faith in Christ no matter what rejection they endured.

✠ *What can I learn from this passage?*

Jesus' Burial (15:42–47)

Shortly before Jesus' death, a woman anoints Jesus with expensive perfume as he dines at the home of a Pharisee. Jesus links the anointing with his death. Those with Jesus during this event who complain about the waste of money will have a new understanding of the anointing. Since Jesus' burial is done in haste with no time for the usual burial procedures, the anointing is indeed preparation for his burial. Jesus' actual burial shows the courage of the renowned council member who requests Jesus' body. Women witness Jesus' burial. It's a time for silent pondering.

✠ *What can I learn from this passage?*

Jesus Is Raised (16:1–8)

Jesus Christ, the Son of God, is raised from the dead. The angel in the empty tomb tells the women to tell the disciples that Jesus has been raised and is going before them to Galilee, which means he is about to lead them into the world. The Good News of Jesus Christ, the Son of God, has reached a conclusion. He has been raised as he said he would be. The disciples must have laughed and hugged as they began to catch a glimmer of all Jesus had tried to teach them. Darkness gives way to light. The power of death was conquered, evil was conquered, and the world had a new beginning.

✠ *What can I learn from this passage?*

The Resurrected Jesus and His Followers (16:9–20; Long Ending)

Jesus' resurrection isn't the end of salvation history. Jesus had to appear to others to confirm his resurrection. Jesus' followers didn't just sit back and discuss how wonderful it is that Jesus has been raised. The story goes on. Jesus commissions his disciples to go out and baptize those who believe. Jesus' ascension completes Jesus' visible mission on Earth. Now the disciples must carry on his message.

✠ *What can I learn from this passage?*

PART 2: INDIVIDUAL STUDY (MARK 14—15:20)

Day 1: Planning Jesus' Death (14:1–11)

It is two days before the Feasts of Passover and Unleavened Bread. These feasts fell on the same day, so the Jews celebrated them as one. The Feast of Unleavened Bread was a celebration of the barley harvest, and people ate unleavened bread throughout the celebration.

The chief priests and scribes seek to arrest and kill Jesus but, fearing a riot, they decide not do it during the feast because a large number of pilgrims will be in Jerusalem. Mark leaves no doubt that Jesus is a hunted man. As Mark has done often throughout the gospel, he introduces one scene, immediately turns his attention to another, and then returns to the first. In this passage, he begins with the chief priests' and Pharisees' plot to kill Jesus, then turns his attention to a second scene. When he finishes the second scene, he will return to the first.

After introducing the plot, Mark turns his attention to a meal at the house of Simon, a man with leprosy in Bethany, a few miles from Jerusalem. Simon was apparently known to the early Church community. As Jesus dines, an unnamed woman anoints Jesus' head with costly ointment. Some claim the woman was Mary Magdalene, but there is no evidence of this.

The story of the anointing identifies Jesus' role as the Messiah and his impending death and burial. Those present become indignant at this apparent waste of good oil, which could have been sold and the money given to the poor. Jesus says the poor will always be with them, and they can find opportunities to help the poor, but Jesus will not always be with his disciples. Jesus isn't denying the need to help the poor, but this is Jesus' hour of salvation and the shadow of the cross looms over these last days. Jesus, knowing he will be buried as a criminal without an anointing, declares that the woman is anointing him for his burial and that her deed will be proclaimed throughout the world.

Mark returns to the chief priests and Pharisees, who are intent on killing Jesus. To their surprise and delight, Judas Iscariot arrives with the intention of handing Jesus over to them. They don't wish to take Jesus before a crowd, but with the help of Judas they can capture Jesus when he is alone with his handful of disciples. Although Mark places the betrayal of Jesus immediately after the anointing, he doesn't tell us the anointing is the motive for Judas' actions.

Mark specifically mentions that Judas was one of the Twelve, a fact that heightens the infamy of the betrayal. Jesus spent a major part of his ministry with his trusted Twelve, and one of them betrays him. Mark gives no reason for Judas' betrayal. When Jewish leaders learn of Judas' willingness to hand Jesus over, they happily promise to pay Judas for doing so.

Lectio Divina

Spend 8 to 10 minutes in silent contemplation of the following passage:

> We can't forget the emotional pain Jesus endured during his passion. Many years ago, a bishop who worked hard for the poor of his diocese in Central America wept when those he counseled and prayed with stormed his house and almost killed him because the dictator paid them. Even during the attack, he was touched by the sadness in their faces. Some of them even wept as they tore his house apart. He told a friend that he would have willingly died at the hands of the dictator rather than see the poor be forced to turn against him. We're aware of Jesus' suffering and death, but we sometimes overlook his emotional pain. His friends betrayed him, denied him, and abandoned him. We're grateful to the woman who gave him a few moments of comfort by anointing his head with expensive perfume. We look with sadness on the pain Jesus accepted for our sins. Sacrificing for Jesus becomes easier when we realize what he endured for us.

✠ *What can I learn from this passage?*

Day 2: The Passover Meal (14:12–31)

In the opening line of this chapter, Mark correctly identifies the Feasts of Passover and Unleavened Bread as beginning at the same time. The Feast of Unleavened Bread was actually celebrated for an entire week. Mark incorrectly places the beginning of the Feast of Unleavened Bread on the day before Passover, as Jesus sends two disciples to prepare for the feast. In the Passover meal, the Hebrew people celebrate their deliverance from

Egypt when the angels killed the firstborn of all Egyptians but passed over the homes of Hebrew people who had the blood of the sacrificed lamb on their doorposts (Exodus 12:23). Passover begins at sundown. On the afternoon before Passover, the paschal lamb is sacrificed and made ready for the Passover meal.

The manner of Jesus' preparation recalls the preparation for Jesus' solemn entrance into Jerusalem. Jesus again takes the initiative, instructing two disciples to follow a man carrying a stone water jar to a house with an upper room where the meal is to be celebrated. They simply tell the owner of the house (as they told the owner of the colt Jesus used for his entry into Jerusalem) that the teacher has need for his property. The owner makes no objection and shows them the upper room, and the disciples prepare for the Passover feast.

Although two disciples should already be in Jerusalem preparing for the feast, Mark portrays Jesus as entering the city in the evening with "the Twelve." The episode points toward the new Israel's replacing the old, and the number Twelve becomes even more significant. Mark is more concerned with the theological message than with the detail that two disciples were already in the upper room. The Twelve—the new Israel—enter Jerusalem to celebrate Passover.

The story jumps to the middle of the meal, when Jesus proclaims solemnly that one apostle will betray him. He declares that the one who dips bread in the same dish with him—the one who shares in the intimacy of table fellowship—will betray him. Jesus again calls himself Son of Man in the sense of the suffering servant and declares that the betrayal was foretold. Although foretold, the act is nevertheless carried out with the free will given to the betrayer by God, and the deed is so treacherous that it would have been better for the betrayer if he'd never been born.

During the meal, Jesus takes the bread, blesses it, breaks it, and gives it to the Twelve saying, "Take it; this is my body." He takes the cup, gives thanks, and gives it to the Twelve, who drink from it. Jesus declares that this cup is the "blood of the covenant," shed not only for the disciples, but for many, meaning "for all." *Blood of the covenant* recalls the blood of the sacrifice that was sprinkled over the people by Moses at Sinai as a sign of the covenant between God and the chosen nation (Exodus 24:8). Jesus is offering himself as the new covenant through his passion, death, and resurrection.

After the disciples partake of Jesus' Body and Blood, Jesus speaks of not drinking of the fruit of the vine (the wine) until he shares it in the kingdom of God. He is apparently speaking about the time of his resurrection. He introduces this statement with "Amen, I say to you," the common expression Jesus uses to strongly underline what he has to say. Jesus is saying that this is his *last supper* before his death and resurrection.

The paschal meal ends with the usual thanksgiving hymn sung at the end of the Passover meal, and Jesus and his disciples leave for the Mount of Olives. Many pilgrims to Jerusalem chose the Mount of Olives as a place of rest during major feasts. Judas, having camped with Jesus and the Twelve on other occasions, would know where they slept.

Lectio Divina

Spend 8 to 10 minutes in silent contemplation of the following passage:

The Passover meal with Jesus never ends. It continues in every celebration of the Eucharist. We partake of the Body and Blood of Christ and are meant to conform our lives to Jesus' life. During the meal, Jesus entered into a new covenant with the new people of God, a covenant we celebrate when we're received into the Body of Christ at baptism. Jesus shows that the gift we received wasn't gained without great suffering and death. We have the security of the new covenant, but we also have the responsibilities that come with this gift. We sit at the banquet with Christ, sharing in his life and sharing his life with others. That is the responsibility we take upon ourselves, the privilege of the meal and the obligation to spread the Good News of Jesus Christ.

✠ *What can I learn from this passage?*

Day 3: The Events in the Garden (14:32–52)

Jesus arrives at a place named Gethsemane. This place, although not easily identified, is thought to be at the foot of the Mount of Olives. Jesus announces that he'll proceed a little further from the group to pray. He chooses Peter, James, and John to accompany him, a choice that points to the moment's importance because they are chosen to be with Jesus at important events of his life. Jesus' agony in the garden most certainly happened as reported, because it would be embarrassing for Mark and Jesus' followers to witness this powerful leader suddenly become a weak and frightened man, as human as themselves. Jesus admits he is sorrowful even to death. Jesus orders the three disciples to remain where they are, keep watch, and remain alert.

Jesus moves forward, falls on the ground, and begs God to have this hour pass from him. This *hour* refers to the time for evil to triumph. This is the only time in the Gospel of Mark that Jesus addresses the Father by the intimate title *Abba*. This name given to the Father by Jesus shows the familiar relationship between Jesus and God the Father. Jesus prays that the "cup" might pass from him. Throughout the Old Testament, the image of "cup" was used for suffering and punishment. But Jesus, true to his call, places himself at the mercy of the divine will. It is the Father's will, not the Son's, that matters at this moment.

When Jesus returns to find the three disciples sleeping, he addresses Peter by the name he had when Jesus first met him. Because Peter doesn't act like a rock at this point, Jesus addresses him as "Simon" and tells him to keep watch to avoid temptation. Peter is open to following Christ and dying for him, but Peter must deal with his weak human nature. Jesus declares that the spirit is willing, but the flesh is weak.

Jesus goes off to pray as he did the first time and returns to find his disciples asleep again. They sheepishly don't know how to answer Jesus when he awakens them. When Jesus returns from prayer a third time and again finds the disciples sleeping, Jesus can do no more; the hour for the power of evil has come. The suffering servant, the Son of Man, is to be betrayed and delivered into the hands of sinners. As much as Jesus prayed that the cup of suffering pass from him, he remains in control of the situation and awakens his disciples so they can meet "the betrayer."

Judas leads a crowd armed with swords and clubs to the area. The crowd is sent by the chief priests, the scribes, and the elders. Mark makes no mention of soldiers, as do the other gospels. The sadness of the betrayal is heightened as Mark writes that Jesus is betrayed by "Judas, one of the Twelve." Judas greets Jesus with a kiss, a sign of intimate friendship, but Jesus says nothing. As Jesus is arrested, someone cuts off the ear of a slave of the high priest.

The mob came after Jesus as though they were coming after a man of violence, but Jesus had preached openly, "day after day" in the Temple, and they did nothing. That Jesus could speak of preaching daily in the Temple area seems to point to a ministry in Jerusalem longer than the one given in the Gospel of Mark.

When Jesus offers himself up in accord with the fulfillment of Scripture, he alludes to a number of Scripture passages rather than one specific passage. As Jesus predicted, he is abandoned by those who promised to remain faithful. The Gospel of Mark alone speaks of the young man who ran away naked. Some believe this young man must have been Mark, since he was the only one who wrote about the incident. This, however, cannot be verified.

Lectio Divina

Spend 8 to 10 minutes in silent contemplation of the following passage:

> Jesus prayed for the cup of suffering to pass from him, but he said, "not what I will but what you will." He knew he had to face the cross as part of his mission to bring salvation. Like the rest of us, Jesus had to abandon himself to God's will at the moment of his death. Peter, James, and John knew something dreadful was about to happen, but they had no idea that Jesus would be hanging on a cross within twenty-four hours. As weak and tired as they were, they fought off sleep for as long as they could, but they remained close to Jesus. They didn't crawl away to a warmer or more comfortable spot. In many ways, we're like Jesus' apostles at this point. We may

not really know how much Jesus depends on us, and we give in to our human weaknesses. We do, however, remain faithful to Jesus despite our weaknesses. Weak as we are, we're there for Jesus, and he knows this.

✠ *What can I learn from this passage?*

Day 4: Jesus Before the Sanhedrin (14:53–72)

As Jesus is led off, the chief priests, elders, and scribes have assembled. Mark comments that Peter follows "at a distance," which indicates some hesitation about his commitment to Jesus. Peter goes into the high priest's courtyard to warm himself at a fire in the presence of some guards. As Mark does so often in his gospel, he turns his attention elsewhere with the intention of returning to Peter at the end of the next narrative. In this way, he links two narratives, contrasting Jesus the faithful one to Peter the weak one. Where Jesus triumphs, Peter fails.

At Jesus' trial, witnesses give false and conflicting testimony, but the Sanhedrin ignore the contradictions. Jesus' trial takes place at night. The accusation is that Jesus said he would destroy the Temple built with hands and in three days build another not made with hands. Readers of the Gospel of Mark would immediately understand that Jesus was referring to himself. He would be entombed and be raised as the Temple of the new covenant. Jesus remains silent in the presence of these false witnesses and refuses to defend himself before the high priest.

In the first line at the beginning of his gospel, Mark declares that he is writing about Jesus the Christ, the Son of God. Now the high priest directly asks Jesus whether he is the Messiah, the Son of the "Blessed One," which means Son of God. Throughout the gospel, Jesus remains silent about his identity. Now, before some members of the Sanhedrin, he openly confesses that he is indeed the Messiah, the Son of God. His strong response, "I am," echoes God's words from the burning bush when God directs Moses to tell the Israelites that "I AM" sent him (Exodus 3:14). Jesus underlines his messianic claim by applying to himself the words of Daniel the prophet, proclaiming that the high priest will see him, Jesus, as the Son of Man sitting at the right hand of God and coming on the clouds of heaven (7:13).

In this statement, Jesus speaks of himself as the triumphant Son of Man instead of the suffering Son of Man. Jesus' words in Mark's Gospel are most likely meant more for the early Church members who believed they, not the high priest, would soon witness the Second Coming of Jesus. The terms *Messiah, Son of God,* and *Son of Man* are used together only at this time in the gospel.

The high priest follows tradition on hearing Jesus proclaim himself as the divine Messiah. He tears his garments as a sign that Jesus has blasphemed. The high priest asks the others what they think after hearing the blasphemy, and they condemn Jesus. No longer do they need witnesses; Jesus' own words condemn him. Although it's unlikely, Mark states that some of the Sanhedrin spit on Jesus, blindfold him, and beat him, challenging him to prophesy for them. The soldiers join in the mockery.

Mark's Gospel returns to Peter in the courtyard and highlights the clear contrast between Peter and Jesus. When one of the high priest's maids accuses Peter of being with Jesus, he denies knowing what she's talking about. Just as Peter moves to the outer court of the Temple, a cock crows. The maid sees him again and says he was one of them, meaning one of Jesus' disciples, but Peter denies her accusation. Later, bystanders accuse him of being one of the disciples, saying the proof is that Peter is a Galilean. Each denial becomes worse than the one before, until Peter finally curses and swears, vehemently proclaiming that he doesn't know Jesus. Where Jesus professed his identity before the Sanhedrin, Peter denies any knowledge of Jesus. When the cock crows a second time, Peter immediately recalls Jesus' words; laden with remorse, Peter breaks into tears.

The disciples of the early Church who denied Christ to avoid suffering or death could find hope in Peter's denial and repentance at this tragic hour.

Lectio Divina

Spend 8 to 10 minutes in silent contemplation of the following passage:

> Peter and Paul are the two great apostles of the early Church. Before they repented and became great saints, one denied Christ and the other persecuted Christians. Many of us struggle to live close to Christ, and we may fail, but failure in living for Christ doesn't

keep us from turning back to him. Jesus remained faithful to his message before the Sanhedrin, knowing they had the power to free him if he would deny his teachings. But he held firm, as Peter did not. Because we know of Jesus' willingness to forgive, we can seek forgiveness and live as stronger Christians. The history of the Church is filled with great saints who once denied Christ but became more dedicated because of their failures.

✠ *What can I learn from this passage?*

Day 5: Jesus Is Condemned to Death (15:1–20)

At daybreak, the Sanhedrin gather to reach a verdict. As the weak suffering servant, Jesus is bound and delivered to Pilate. Although Pilate, the procurator, is known to the Jewish people as a treacherous ruler who would ordinarily have little remorse about killing anyone, Mark presents a different picture of him. While the religious leaders' concern centered on Jesus' claim to be God and Messiah, as a political ruler Pilate is more concerned about Jesus' claim of being a king. Ironically, Pilate is right when he asks Jesus if he is the king of the Jews, but Jesus' kingdom is not of this world. Jesus has no way of answering this question directly without being misunderstood. He reminds Pilate that Pilate was the one who said this. It's ironic that throughout the passion, the Romans will be the ones to truly identify Jesus. Pilate presses Jesus further about the leaders' accusations. To his amazement, Jesus remains silent. The prophet Isaiah, in writing about the suffering servant who was to come, spoke of Jesus as a silent lamb before the slaughterer (53:7).

Mark notes that it was a custom at festival time to release whichever prisoner the crowd wanted. This custom is recorded nowhere in the records of the era except in the gospels. Pilate, recognizing Jesus' innocence and knowing the chief priests had handed him over with little evidence, asks who the crowd wants released, Jesus or Barabbas. The religious leaders incite the crowd to call for the release of Barabbas, a political prisoner who had murdered people during a riot. In response to the cry of the people, Pilate releases Barabbas. Mark notes that Pilate again refers to Jesus as King of the Jews. When Pilate asks what he must do with Jesus, the crowd shouts, "Crucify him." When Pilate asks what evil Jesus has done, the crowd ignores the question and continues to shout "Crucify him!" Pilate has Jesus flogged and hands him over to the soldiers.

The irony continues as the soldiers lead Jesus into a courtyard, most likely in Pilate's palace in Jerusalem, where they mock him as King of the Jews. They place on his shoulders a robe of purple, the color of royalty, and force a crown of thorns onto his head. They spit on him, strike his head with a reed, and mockingly pay homage to him. Jesus' kingship is thus identified by Mark as one of suffering and servanthood. The soldiers strip Jesus of the purple cloak, clothe him with his own clothes, and lead him out for crucifixion.

Lectio Divina

Spend 8 to 10 minutes in silent contemplation of the following passage:

Although some people of Jesus' day called for his crucifixion, we cannot view this sin as tainting all people of Judea. Among the crowd, some wept out of concern for Jesus while others, stirred up by their trusted religious leaders, believed Jesus was a criminal and joined in the call for his crucifixion. We can learn from this event: Whenever we sin, we call out for Barabbas and don't care that Jesus was crucified for our sins. The passion continues as Jesus is ridiculed and mocked by the soldiers, who don't realize they're mocking the king of the universe. Jesus' endurance during his passion tells us a great deal about God's love.

✠ *What can I learn from this passage?*

Review Questions

1. What is the significance of Jesus' anointing at Bethany?

2. Why do the chief priests need Judas's help to capture Jesus?

3. What is significant about the apostles' preparation of the Passover meal?

4. What does Jesus say about Judas's betrayal?

5. What does Jesus do at the Last Supper?

6. What insights about Peter do we gain when we see how courageously he proclaims that he will die with Christ?

7. What happens to Jesus during his agony in the garden?

8. Why do Jesus' disciples have difficulty staying awake during Jesus' agony in the garden?

9. How does Judas betray Jesus?

10. What is the charge against Jesus when he's brought before the Sanhedrin?

11. What do we learn about Peter from his denial of Jesus?

About the Author

William A. Anderson, DMin, PhD, is a presbyter of the diocese of Wheeling-Charleston, West Virginia. Director of retreats and parish missions, professor, catechist, spiritual director, and former pastor, he has written extensively on pastoral, spiritual, and religious subjects. Father Anderson earned his doctor of ministry degree from St. Mary's Seminary & University in Baltimore and his doctorate in sacred theology from Duquesne University in Pittsburgh.

ALSO AVAILABLE IN THE
LIGUORI CATHOLIC BIBLE STUDY SERIES

Introduction to the Bible:
Overview, Historical Context, and Cultural Perspectives
ISBN 978-0-7648-2119-6 • 112 pages

The Gospel of Matthew: Proclaiming the Ministry of Jesus
ISBN 978-0-7648-2120-2 • 160 pages

Words of Praise for
INTRODUCTION TO THE BIBLE

"This very useful catechetical work, *Introduction to the Bible*, provides an excellent and very accessible introduction to the study of sacred Scripture. With the explanation and introduction to *lectio divina*, the reader will discover praying the Scriptures as an important spiritual practice. I am certain this text will be very useful to young people and adults who wish to learn about sacred Scripture, the history of salvation it makes known to us, and the cultural and historical context of its many books."

MOST REVEREND MICHAEL J. BRANSFIELD, BISHOP OF WHEELING-CHARLESTON

The Gospel of Luke: Salvation for All Humanity
ISBN 978-0-7648-2122-6 • 144 pages

The Gospel of John: The Word Became Flesh
ISBN 978-0-7648-2123-3 • 144 pages

For more information,
call 800-325-9521 or visit liguori.org